ALL-TIME-FAVORITE RECIPES From MISSOURI COOKS

Dedication

For every cook who wants to create amazing recipes from the great state of Missouri.

Appreciation

Thanks to all our Missouri cooks who shared their delightful and delicious recipes with us!

Gooseberry Patch
An imprint of Globe Pequot
246 Goose Lane
Guilford, CT 06437
www.gooseberrypatch.com
1 800 854 6673

978-162093-397-8

Printed in Korea.

Do you have a tried & true recipe...tip, craft or memory that you'd like to see featured in a *Gooseberry Patch* cookbook? Visit our website at www.gooseberrypatch.com and follow the easy steps to submit your favorite family recipe.

Or send them to us at:

Gooseberry Patch
PO Box 812
Columbus, OH 43216-0812

Don't forget to include the number of servings your recipe makes, plus your name, address, phone number and email address. If we select your recipe, your name will appear right along with it... and you'll receive a FREE copy of the book!

MISSOURI COOKS

ICONIC MISSOURI

Missouri's history flourishes with influence from American Indian, Spanish, French, African-American and more! The Pony Express, Oregon Trail, Santa Fe Trail and California Trail all began in Missouri and so it is no surprise that The Gateway Arch, the tallest man-made monument in the United States, is located in St. Louis and represents Missouri's role as the "Gateway to the West."

The variety in cultures has allowed for some of the most delicious and diverse cuisines to derive from Missouri. And as a state that recognizes the significance in having a State Grape, the Norton/Cynthiana grape, it's no wonder Missouri has some of the finest cooks around!

Whether it's the writings of Mark Twain, folk music, canyons, caves or ice cream cones (which made their debut at the St. Louis World's Fair in 1904) that you love about Missouri, this state has it all along with a delicious history of recipes to go with it! The amazing cooks from the "Show-Me State" have shared recipes that are dear to their hearts.

You'll find everything from Slow-Cooker Honey Ribs, Grilled Salami Pizza Sandwiches and Sarah's Southwestern Breakfast Casserole to Saint Louis Gooey Butter Cake, Shrimp & Crab Layered Dip and more! We know you will love this collection of tried & true recipes from cooks from all around the great state of Missouri. Enjoy!

OUR STORY

Back in 1984, our families were neighbors in little Delaware, Ohio. With small children, we wanted to do what we loved and stay home with the kids too. We had always shared a love of home cooking and so, **Gooseberry Patch** was born.

Almost immediately, we found a connection with our customers and it wasn't long before these friends started sharing recipes. Since then we've enjoyed publishing hundreds of cookbooks with your tried & true recipes.

We know we couldn't have done it without our friends all across the country and we look forward to continuing to build a community with you. Welcome to the **Gooseberry Patch** family!

JoAnn & Vickie

TABLE OF CONTENTS

CHAPTER ONE

Prairie-Perfect Breakfast

ENJOY THESE TASTY BREAKFAST RECIPES THAT BRING YOU TO THE TABLE WITH A HEARTY "GOOD MORNING!" AND CARRY YOU THROUGH THE DAY TO TACKLE WHATEVER COMES YOUR WAY.

PENNY'S PANCAKES

PENNY SHERMAN,
AVA, MO

Ditch the pancake mix and for good. These pancakes are so good, they don't eeven need syrup!

2 c. all-purpose flour
1/2 c. sugar
4-1/2 t. baking powder
1 t. salt
2 eggs, beaten
2 c. milk
1/4 c. butter, melted and slightly cooled
Optional: 1/2 c. blueberries, white chocolate chips or chopped pecans
Garnish: butter, pancake syrup or whipped cream

In a large bowl, combine flour, sugar, baking powder and salt; mix well and set aside. In a separate bowl, whisk together eggs, milk and melted butter. Add egg mixture to flour mixture; stir until all big lumps are gone. Stir in optional ingredients, if desired. Spoon batter onto a greased hot griddle by 1/4 cupfuls. Cook until golden on both sides. Serve topped with butter, syrup or whipped cream. Leftover pancakes freeze well.

Makes 12 5-inch pancakes

HANNA'S FAVORITE FRENCH TOAST

HANNA DONNER
GRANDVIEW, MO

My mother taught me this recipe when I was young...I still love it!

In a shallow dish, beat eggs with milk, sugar, cinnamon and vanilla; set aside. Melt half of butter in a skillet over medium heat. Dip 2 bread slices in egg mixture, coating well on both sides; add to skillet. Cook for about 2 minutes, until golden; turn and cook other side. Repeat with remaining butter and bread. Serve slices topped with peanut butter and maple syrup; sprinkle with powdered sugar.

Serves 4

2 eggs, beaten
2 T. milk
1/2 c. sugar
1 t. cinnamon
1 t. vanilla extract
1 T. butter, divided
4 slices honey wheat bread
Garnish: creamy peanut butter, maple syrup, powdered sugar

KITCHEN TIP

A crock of honey butter...so yummy on warm bread, biscuits and muffins. Simply blend together 1/2 cup each of honey and softened butter.

BUTTERSCOTCH BUBBLES

JOYCE KEELING
SPRINGFIELD, MO

I received this recipe from a pen pal when I was just ten years old. It was the first recipe that I made by myself, and I was thrilled that my family liked it so much. Whenever company arrived, Mom would tell me, "Go make some of your bubbles." I was so proud when I served them...after just one taste, they'd ask for my recipe!

1/4 c. butter, melted
1/4 c. brown sugar, packed
1/4 c. chopped nuts
1/2 t. cinnamon
8-oz. tube refrigerated biscuits, quartered

Place melted butter in a shallow dish; set aside. In a shallow dish, mix together brown sugar, nuts and cinnamon. Dip biscuit pieces into butter, then into brown sugar mixture. Arrange biscuits on ungreased baking sheets. Bake at 475 degrees for 10 minutes, or until lightly golden. Serve warm.

Makes 3-1/2 dozen pieces

BUTTERMILK COFFEE CAKE

CHERYL GRAY
WARRENTON, MO

Recently I came across my mom's handwritten recipe for coffee cake. Sometimes, if we had a snow day from school, Mom would make it for my brother and me. Its wonderful aroma filled the house. Now I make it for my husband and me, and when I go home to visit my dad, I always make a couple to freeze and take to him. It is one of the few recipes I can make that taste just like Mom used to make.

1 c. raisins
2 c. boiling water
4 c. all-purpose flour
2 c. sugar
1-1/2 t. cinnamon
1/2 c. shortening
1/2 t. salt
2 t. baking soda
2 c. buttermilk

Combine raisins and boiling water. Let stand for 10 minutes; drain. In a large bowl, mix together flour, sugar and cinnamon; cut in shortening with a fork. Set aside 1/3 cup of mixture for topping. Add salt, baking soda, buttermilk and raisins. Mix well; batter will be thick. Divide batter evenly between 2 greased and floured 9" round cake pans. Sprinkle reserved topping over batter. Bake at 375 degrees for 35 minutes, or until cake tests done with a toothpick inserted in the center. Cool for about 10 minutes; remove from pan. Serve immediately, or wrap in aluminum foil. May be frozen. To serve, cut into slices.

Makes 2 coffee cakes

CHRISTMAS BREAKFAST CASSEROLE

MAGGIE CLARK
KANSAS CITY, MO

For as long as I can remember, this dish has been my go-to recipe for Christmas morning brunch. Served with a mixed fruit salad, coffee cake and mimosas, it gives the whole family a hearty start before the frantic unwrapping of packages begins.

8-oz. tube refrigerated crescent rolls
8-oz. pkg. brown & serve pork sausage links, sliced
2 c. shredded Swiss cheese
4 eggs, lightly beaten
3/4 c. milk
1 T. green pepper, diced
1 T. red pepper, diced
1/2 t. dried oregano
1/2 t. salt
1/2 t. pepper

Separate crescent rolls into 2 large rectangles; place in an ungreased 13"x9" baking pan. Press over the bottom and 1/2-inch up the sides to form a crust. Arrange sliced sausages over crust; top with cheese. Combine remaining ingredients in a bowl; whisk well and pour over cheese. Bake, uncovered, at 425 degrees for 20 to 25 minutes, until golden.

Serves 5 to 6

JUST FOR FUN

Saint Joseph, Missouri was the starting point of the famed Pony Express.

PECAN FLAPJACKS

KELLY HALL
BUTLER, MO

These tender pancakes have been a part of my family's traditional Christmas breakfast ever since my cousin in Estes Park, Colorado gave me this recipe years ago.

- **1-1/2 c. whole-wheat flour**
- **1 c. all-purpose flour**
- **1 c. long-cooking oats, uncooked**
- **1/2 c. yellow cornmeal**
- **1 T. baking powder**
- **2 t. baking soda**
- **1 t. salt**
- **3/4 c. chilled butter, diced**
- **4 eggs, beaten**
- **4 c. buttermilk**
- **1/2 c. honey**
- **1 c. chopped pecans**

Process flours, oats, cornmeal, baking powder, baking soda and salt together in a food processor until well blended. Add butter; process until mixture resembles coarse meal and set aside. Whisk eggs and buttermilk together in a large bowl; whisk in honey. Stir in flour mixture; fold in nuts. Drop by 1/4 cupfuls onto a preheated, well greased griddle; cook until golden on both sides.

Serves 8 to 10

CRANBERRY NUT BREAD

PAULA WILSON
COLUMBIA, MO

I grew up attending a small rural church where it was customary to go caroling the week before Christmas. The best part was always returning to the church, where we warmed up with cups of hot chocolate and some of the best fruit breads and cookies ever made! My mother's Cranberry Nut Bread was always a favorite.

2 c. all-purpose flour
1 c. sugar
1-1/2 t. baking powder
1/2 t. baking soda
1 t. salt
1 t. orange zest
1 egg, beaten
2 T. oil
3/4 c. orange juice
1-1/4 c. cranberries, chopped
1/2 c. chopped pecans

Combine flour, sugar, baking powder, baking soda, salt and zest in a large bowl. Beat together egg, oil and juice in a separate bowl; add to dry ingredients and mix well. Stir in berries and nuts; set aside. Grease the bottom only of one, 9"x5" loaf pan loaf pans. Pour batter into pans. Bake at 350 degrees, one hour for a regular loaf. Turn out bread and cool on a wire rack.

Makes one loaf

HOLIDAY FRENCH TOAST BAKE

THERESA ELDRIDGE
FESTUS, MO

My mom showed her love through cooking. Every Christmas, she would have something delicious baking while we all opened gifts by the big fireplace in the living room. We still keep our Christmas breakfast tradition even though she has passed away...it is a great way to keep her memory with us. This casserole has become a family favorite, and I hope you love it as much as we do. I make this often!

1 loaf day-old French bread, cut into one-inch cubes
Optional: 1 to 2 c. fresh cranberries or blueberries
8 eggs, beaten
2-1/2 c. milk
1/2 c. sugar
2 T. cinnamon
2 T. vanilla extract
Optional: pancake syrup, or fresh fruit, honey and powdered sugar

Place bread cubes in a greased 13"x9" baking pan. Sprinkle with berries, if using; set aside. In a bowl, whisk together remaining ingredients except optional garnish. Pour over bread cubes, covering well. Cover and refrigerate for several hours or overnight. To bake, uncover pan; stir to make sure bread cubes are coated evenly. If desired, pour Optional Topping over all. Set pan on a baking sheet to catch any drips. Bake, uncovered, at 350 degrees for 40 to 50 minutes. Garnish as desired.

OPTIONAL TOPPING:

1-1/3 c. brown sugar, packed
3/4 c. butter, sliced
3 T. light corn syrup

Optional Topping:
Combine all ingredients in a saucepan over medium heat. Cook and stir until boiling and brown sugar is dissolved.

Serves 6 to 8

MUSHROOM & HERB OMELET

PENNY SHERMAN
AVA, MO

Don't worry if the omelet splits or tears as the edges are lifted... the cheese topping will make it look and taste delicious!

- **2 eggs**
- **1-1/2 t. fresh parsley, snipped**
- **1/2 t. fresh thyme, basil or chives, snipped**
- **salt and pepper to taste**
- **3/4 c. sliced mushrooms**
- **2 t. butter, divided**
- **1 to 2 T. shredded Swiss or Cheddar cheese**

Whisk together eggs, herbs, salt and pepper in a small bowl; set aside. In a small skillet over medium heat, sauté mushrooms in one teaspoon butter until tender, 3 to 4 minutes. Transfer mushrooms to a separate bowl; cover and set aside. Melt remaining butter in skillet; pour egg mixture into skillet. Cook over medium-low heat, lifting edge gently with a spatula to allow uncooked portion to flow underneath. When almost set, spoon mushrooms onto one half of the omelet; fold over omelet. Sprinkle with cheese; let stand one to 2 minutes until cheese melts. Slide onto a plate.

Serves 1

CRESCENT BREAKFAST CASSEROLE

TAMMY WALKER
KANSAS CITY, MO

This is a quick & easy breakfast casserole for a chilly morning or a hearty, filling supper.

- **8-oz. tube refrigerated crescent rolls**
- **6 to 8 eggs, beaten**
- **1/4 c. milk**
- **3/4 c. finely shredded Cheddar cheese**
- **1/2 c. bacon or ground pork sausage, cooked and crumbled**
- **salt and pepper to taste**

Line the bottom and sides of a lightly greased 13"x9" baking pan with unrolled crescents, pinching seams together to seal. In a bowl, mix together remaining ingredients. Pour over dough in baking pan. Bake at 350 degrees for about 20 minutes, until golden and center is set.

Serves 8

YUMMY BLUEBERRY WAFFLES

RITA MORGAN
SPRINGFIELD, MO

When I was a little girl, my grandpa owned a blueberry farm. The berries were so delicious that we always took home several gallons when our summer visit was over. This waffle recipe cooks up nice and fluffy...and the farm-fresh blueberries only make them better!

2 eggs
2 c. all-purpose flour
1-3/4 c. milk
1/2 c. oil
1 T. sugar
4 t. baking powder
1/4 t. salt
1/2 t. vanilla extract
1 to 1-1/2 c. blueberries

In a large bowl, beat eggs with an electric mixer on medium speed until fluffy. Add remaining ingredients except berries; beat just until smooth. Spray a waffle iron with non-stick vegetable spray. Pour batter by 1/2 cupfuls onto the preheated waffle iron. Scatter desired amount of berries over batter. Bake according to manufacturer's directions, until golden.

Makes 4

PRESENTATION

You're never too old for party favors! Send your guests home with a whimsical memento...tiny potted plants, little bags of homemade candy, mini photo frames or even bubbles.

SWEET FRUIT & ALMOND SCONES

BARB SCHOENHOLTZ
REEDS SPRING, MO

When I bake these scones, they bring back memories of good times and my kids enjoying them with fresh butter and jam. Delicious!

2 c. all-purpose flour
1/4 c. sugar, divided
1 T. baking powder
1/2 t. salt
6 T. chilled butter, diced
2 eggs, lightly beaten
1/2 c. plus 1 T. whipping cream, divided
1/2 c. dried cranberries, blueberries, cherries or mixed berries
1/2 c. sliced toasted almonds
Garnish: butter, jam, whipped cream

In a large bowl, sift together flour, 3 tablespoons sugar, baking powder and salt; set aside. Use a fork or pastry blender to cut in butter until very small pieces form. Make a well in the center; set aside. In a separate bowl, whisk eggs and 1/2 cup cream together. Pour egg mixture into well in flour mixture. Stir lightly with a fork until dough comes together. Add berries and nuts; mix together. Turn out dough onto a lightly floured surface. With floured hands, gently pat dough into an 8-inch circle, about 3/8-inch thick. Cut circle into 8 wedges; transfer to a parchment paper-lined baking sheet. Brush tops with remaining cream and sprinkle with remaining sugar. Bake at 400 degrees for 15 to 20 minutes, until golden. Cool on a wire rack. Serve scones topped with butter, jam and whipped cream.

Makes 8 to 10

RICH ED'S BISCUIT & GRAVY SCRAMBLE

SHERI KOHL
WENTZVILLE, MO

My husband Rich loves his biscuits & gravy and mixes everything together on his plate. I came up with the perfect casserole which includes all his favorite ingredients already mixed together! When I took this dish to a church group brunch, I was overwhelmed with requests by women wanting to make it for their husbands too.

1 lb. ground pork breakfast sausage
2-3/4 oz. pkg. country sausage gravy mix
16.3-oz. tube refrigerated jumbo biscuits, quartered
1 c. shredded Cheddar cheese
6 eggs
1/2 c. milk
salt and pepper to taste

Brown sausage in a skillet over medium heat; drain well. Prepare gravy mix according to package directions; set aside. Spread biscuit quarters in the bottom of a 13"x9" baking pan sprayed with non-stick vegetable spray. Sprinkle with sausage and cheese. Beat together eggs, milk, salt and pepper; pour over ingredients in pan. Pour gravy over all. Bake, uncovered, at 350 degrees for 30 to 45 minutes, until hot and bubbly.

Serves 8

BUTTERSCOTCH SCONES

MARY BETTUCHY
SAINT ROBERT, MO

My mother and I enjoy going out to breakfast together. At one restaurant, we were served butterscotch scones with the meal, and we loved them! I decided to devise my own recipe for them, so we could enjoy a warm butterscotch scone more often.

1 egg, beaten
1/3 c. whipping cream
1/4 c. buttermilk
1 t. vanilla extract
2 c. all-purpose flour
1/3 c. plus 1 T. sugar, divided
2 t. baking powder
1/4 t. salt
6 T. chilled butter, cut into 1-inch pieces
11-oz. pkg. butterscotch baking chips

In a bowl, whisk together egg, cream, buttermilk and vanilla; set aside. In a large bowl, combine flour, 1/3 cup sugar, baking powder and salt. Cut in butter with a pastry cutter until it resembles coarse crumbs. Stir in butterscotch chips. Add buttermilk mixture to flour mixture; stir gently just until mixture starts to come together. Turn out onto a lightly floured work surface; knead gently until a stiff dough forms. Pat dough into a circle, about 7 inches in diameter and one inch thick. Cut circle into 8 wedges. Transfer wedges to a parchment-lined baking sheet; sprinkle tops with remaining sugar. Place on center rack in oven. Bake at 375 degrees for 20 to 30 minutes, until golden and a toothpick inserted in the center comes out with a few crumbs attached. Serve warm.

Makes 8 scones

WILDERNESS BREAKFAST

TAMMY ADAM
LATHROP, MO

This recipe was handed down from my Great-Uncle Russell. He used to cook this breakfast dish while camping on long hunting trips with his sons. My own daughters have used this recipe for 4-H demonstrations and been very successful with it. It can be prepared the night before, refrigerated and baked the next morning.

- **3 c. croutons**
- **1-1/2 c. shredded Cheddar cheese**
- **6 to 8 eggs, beaten**
- **3 c. milk**
- **10-3/4 oz. can cream of chicken soup**
- **3/4 t. dried, minced onion**
- **3/4 t. dry mustard**
- **3/4 t. salt**
- **1/8 t. pepper**
- **1 lb. bacon, crisply cooked and crumbled**
- **1 lb. ground pork sausage, browned and drained**

Line a greased 13"x9" baking pan with croutons and cheese; set aside. In a large bowl, stir together eggs, milk, soup, onion, mustard, salt and pepper. Pour mixture over croutons and cheese; sprinkle with bacon and sausage. Bake, uncovered, for one hour at 325 degrees.

Serves 6 to 8

HAM & CHEESE QUICHE

MELISSA RUSHING
ROGERSVILLE, MO

Great for breakfast or brunch...easy, quick and everyone loves it!

- **1-1/4 c. biscuit baking mix**
- **1/4 c. butter, softened**
- **2 T. boiling water**
- **1 c. cooked ham, diced**
- **1 c. shredded Cheddar or Colby Jack cheese**
- **1/4 c. onion, diced**
- **1-1/2 c. milk**
- **3 eggs, beaten**
- **1/2 t. salt**
- **1/4 t. paprika**

Stir baking mix and butter together until well blended. Add boiling water and stir to make a soft dough. Press into bottom and up sides of a greased 9" pie plate. Sprinkle ham, cheese and onion over dough. Whisk together milk, eggs, salt and paprika until well blended; pour into crust. Bake at 400 degrees for 35 to 40 minutes, until golden and center is set.

Serves 6 to 8

FAMILY-TIME CONVERSATION

The first successful parachute jump from a moving plane was made above the Jefferson Barracks military post, near Saint Louis, in 1912. U.S. Army Captain Albert Berry climbed to 1,500 feet in a Benoist aircraft before positioning himself on a trapeze bar attached to the front of the plane. Air & Space magazine reports Berry saying, "Never again! I believe I turned five somersaults on my way down ... My course downward ... was like a crazy arrow." Berry completed his second jump on March 10.

SARAH'S SOUTHWESTERN BREAKFAST CASSEROLE

MARIAN FORCK
CHAMOIS, MO

Our daughter Sarah made this for Christmas breakfast and it was a big hit, simple and delicious. Prepare it the night before and let it cook while you wait for Santa to come... ready in the morning. We made scrambled eggs and spooned the casserole on top.

4 redskin potatoes, diced

1-1/2 c. cooked ham, cubed

1 onion, diced

1 red pepper, diced

1 T. olive oil

14-1/2 oz. can diced tomatoes

4-oz. can sliced mushrooms, drained

salt and pepper to taste

1/4 c. shredded Cheddar cheese

Optional: additional shredded cheese, sour cream, salsa

Spray a 4-quart slow cooker with non-stick vegetable spray. Layer potatoes, ham, onion and red pepper; drizzle with olive oil. Add tomatoes with juice, mushrooms and seasonings. Cover and cook on low setting for 8 to 9 hours. Just before serving, top with cheese; garnish as desired.

Serves 6

CHERRY-ALMOND COFFEE CAKE

PENNY SHERMAN
AVA, MO

With this terrific recipe, I can serve up a sweet, warm coffee cake to guests in no time at all!

12-oz. tube refrigerated cinnamon rolls
1 c. cherry pie filling
1/4 t. almond extract
1 T. sliced almonds

Separate rolls; set aside icing. Cut each roll into 4 pieces. Place rolls cinnamon-side down in a greased 9" round cake pan. Combine pie filling and extract in a small bowl; spoon over rolls. Sprinkle with almonds. Bake at 375 degrees for 25 to 35 minutes, until golden. Cool in pan for 3 minutes. Cover pan with a wire rack; turn rack and pan over. Remove pan. Place a serving plate upside-down over coffee cake; turn right-side up. Drizzle icing over coffee cake. Cut into wedges to serve.

Serves 6

SO-EASY CARAMEL ROLLS

AMY TEETS
SAINT PETERS, MO

A simple breakfast I like serving to company! If you wish, sprinkle chopped nuts on top of the ice cream topping before adding the rolls.

1/4 c. butter
12-1/4 oz. jar caramel ice cream topping
2 8-oz. tubes refrigerated crescent rolls

Place butter in a 13"x9" baking pan and place in a 375-degree oven until melted. Once melted, add ice cream topping and mix well. Without unrolling the dough, remove dough from tubes. Cut each section into 6 rolls and place cut-side down in pan. Bake at 375 degrees for 20 to 25 minutes. Immediately invert onto a serving plate.

Makes one dozen

NUTTY BROWN SUGAR MUFFINS

PEARL WEAVER
EAST PRAIRIE, MO

With a flavor that's so much like pecan pie, these muffins are sure to become a new favorite.

2 eggs, beaten
1/2 c. butter, melted and cooled slightly
1 c. brown sugar, packed
1/2 c. all-purpose flour
1 c. chopped pecans

Stir together eggs and butter. Add remaining ingredients; stir just until blended. Spray foil muffin cup liners with non-stick vegetable spray. Place liners in a muffin tin; fill 2/3 full. Bake at 350 degrees for 25 minutes. Remove muffins from pan immediately; cool.

Makes 10

HAM SKILLET BREAKFAST

BARBARA BLEDSOE
SAINT LOUIS, MO

Super quick...you don't even have to peel the potatoes!

2 potatoes, cubed
1 onion, chopped
2 to 3 T. oil
1 green pepper, chopped
1 zucchini, chopped
2 c. cooked ham, diced
1 tomato, diced
1/2 c. shredded Cheddar cheese

In a large skillet over medium-high heat, cook potatoes and onion in oil for 5 minutes, or until golden. Add green pepper and zucchini. Cook for 5 additional minutes, until tender. Add ham and tomato; sprinkle with cheese. Cover and cook for 3 to 5 minutes, until heated through and cheese melts.

Serves 4

CINNAMON-APPLE BREAKFAST CAKE

KATY WEDEPOHL
SAINT LOUIS, MO

I once read a recipe for a chocolate-cherry cake that called for just a few ingredients...later I realized I could use the same principles with different ingredients. The Cinnamon-Apple Breakfast Cake was born!

18-1/2 oz. pkg. yellow cake mix
2 eggs, beaten
1 t. vanilla extract
2 t. cinnamon
21-oz. can apple pie filling

ALMOND GLAZE
2 c. powdered sugar
1 t. almond extract
1 to 2 t. milk 2 c. powdered sugar
1 t. almond extract
1 to 2 t. milk

In a bowl, blend dry cake mix, eggs, vanilla and cinnamon; fold in pie filling. Pour into a greased 13"x9" baking pan. Bake, uncovered, at 350 degrees for 35 to 45 minutes, or until a toothpick inserted in center comes out clean. Cool; drizzle with Almond Glaze.

Almond Glaze:
In a small bowl, combine all ingredients; mix well.

Serves 10 to 12

JUST FOR FUN

Aunt Jemima pancake flour was invented in Saint Louis in 1889. It was the first ready-mix food to ever be sold commercially. Take that, Betty Crocker!

TEX-MEX EGG PUFFS

CAROL CREED
BATTLEFIELD, MO

I experimented with the ingredients until this recipe was just right! Mix, bake and serve. How easy is that?

- 1 doz. eggs, beaten
- 2 4-oz. cans chopped green chiles, drained
- 1/2 c. butter, melted and cooled slightly
- 1/2 c. all-purpose flour
- 1 t. baking powder
- 1/2 t. salt
- 16-oz. pkg. shredded Monterey Jack cheese
- 16-oz. container small-curd cottage cheese

In a large bowl, whisk together all ingredients. Spoon into a greased 13"x9" baking pan. Bake, uncovered, at 350 degrees for 35 to 40 minutes, until set. Cut into squares.

Serves 8 to 10

KITCHEN TIP

For hosting a stress-free brunch, focus on make-ahead meals like baked frenh toast and egg casseroles. Save recipes that need to be cooked on the spot, like pancakes and omlets for smaller family breakfasts.

AUNT KORNYE'S CINNAMON ROLLS

RUBY KELSEY
HOLTS SUMMIT, MO

This recipe was found in my great-great-aunt Kornye's handwritten recipe book. At the bottom of the card she wrote "May increase waist size."

3 envs. active dry yeast
2-1/2 c. warm water
4-1/2 c. all-purpose flour
18-1/2 oz. pkg. white cake mix
powdered sugar for dusting
1 c. butter, softened
1 c. brown sugar, packed
1/4 c. cinnamon
16-oz. container cream cheese icing

Dissolve yeast in very warm water, 110 to 115 degrees. Add flour and dry cake mix; stir and knead until smooth. Transfer to a greased bowl; cover with a tea towel and let rise until double in bulk, about 1-1/2 hours. Punch dough down, cover and let rise again until double in bulk, another hour. Roll out dough 1/2-inch thick on a surface dusted with powdered sugar; cut into 2 rectangles. Combine butter, brown sugar and cinnamon; spread equally over each rectangle. Roll up jelly-roll style, starting with a long end. Slice into 2-inch-thick slices. Place on a greased baking sheet and let rise for 30 minutes. Bake at 375 degrees for 20 minutes, or until golden. Cool slightly; spread with icing.

Makes 10 to 15

STREUSEL-TOPPED COFFEE CAKE

PENNY SHERMAN
AVA, MO

Share this tender cake with friends before setting off for a day of shopping.

1-3/4 c. biscuit baking mix, divided
3/4 c. sugar
1/2 c. vanilla yogurt
1 egg, beaten
1 t. vanilla extract
1/4 c. brown sugar, packed
1/2 t. cinnamon

Coat a slow cooker with non-stick vegetable spray. Cut a circle of parchment paper to fit the bottom of the crock; press into place and spray again. In a bowl, mix 1-1/2 cups biscuit mix, sugar, yogurt, egg and vanilla until well blended; set aside. In a small bowl, mix brown sugar, cinnamon and remaining biscuit mix. Spoon half of batter into slow cooker; sprinkle half of brown sugar mixture on top. Repeat layers. Place 2 paper towels on top of slow cooker to absorb condensation. Cover and cook on high setting for 1-3/4 to 2 hours, until a toothpick inserted in the center tests clean. Let coffee cake stand in crock for 10 minutes. Turn out onto a plate; peel off parchment paper. Turn cake over again onto a serving platter, so streusel is on top.

Drizzle:

DRIZZLE
1/2 c. powdered sugar
1 to 2 T. milk

Whisk together powdered sugar and milk, adding enough milk to form a drizzling consistency. Drizzle glaze over coffee cake.

Serves 8

CHAPTER TWO

Piled Gateway-High Salads & Sides

TOSS TOGETHER GREAT TASTE AND HEALTHY GOODNESS TO MAKE FRESH, SATISFYING AND TASTY SALADS THAT ARE PACKED WITH FULL-ON FLAVOR.

MARIAN'S CORN FRITTERS

MARIAN FORCK
CHAMOIS, MO

This has become a family favorite whenever we have a fish fry. If I don't serve them, people will ask me, why not? Everyone loves them! For a large crowd of 40 or more, I will triple the recipe.

1 c. all-purpose flour
2 T. cornstarch
1-1/2 t. baking powder
1 t. salt
2/3 c. water
Optional: several drops yellow food coloring
15-1/2 oz. can corn, drained
oil for deep frying

In a large bowl, combine all ingredients except oil; beat until smooth. Heat several inches of oil to about 365 degrees in a heavy saucepan. Working in batches, drop batter by teaspoonfuls into hot oil. Cook until lightly golden; drain on paper towels.

Makes 20 fritters

MASHED POTATO SALAD

SANDY PITTMAN
GRANBY, MO

We used to have this potato salad when I was a girl at home. It's loved and requested by family & friends alike...a quick and delicious way to use up leftover mashed potatoes.

4 c. cold mashed potatoes
3/4 c. mayonnaise-style salad dressing
1/3 c. mustard
1/2 c. onion, diced
4 to 5 dill pickles, diced
5 eggs, hard-boiled, peeled and chopped

Place mashed potatoes in a large bowl. Add salad dressing and mustard; stir together. Stir in onion and pickles; gently fold in eggs. Cover and chill until serving time.

Serves 6 to 8

MOM'S CANDIED SWEET POTATOES

NAOMI TOWNSEND
OZARK, MO

Growing up on the farm, I had 15 first cousins who all lived in the area, so family gatherings were always a great celebration! My mother's candied sweet potatoes were a favorite treat. If you're not feeding a crowd, this recipe is easy to cut in half.

8 sweet potatoes
1 c. butter
1 c. evaporated milk or half-and-half
2 c. brown sugar, packed
2 t. salt
6 c. mini marshmallows

Scrub potatoes, but do not peel. Place potatoes in a large stockpot; add just enough water to cover. Bring to a boil over high heat. Reduce heat to low. Cover and simmer for 20 to 25 minutes, until fork-tender. Drain; cool slightly and slip off skins. Cut potatoes into 1/2-inch slices; arrange in a buttered 13"x9" baking pan. Melt butter in a saucepan over medium heat; stir in milk or half-and-half, brown sugar and salt. Cook, stirring often, until bubbly and brown sugar is dissolved. Pour over potatoes. Cover and bake at 375 degrees for 20 to 30 minutes, until heated through. Remove from oven; uncover and stir gently. Spread marshmallows evenly on top. Bake, uncovered, about 15 minutes longer, until marshmallows are puffed and golden.

Serves 12 to 16

LYNN'S NUTTY SLAW

LYNN FOLEY
BRANSON, MO

This slaw may sound a little unusual, but it's delicious, oh-so easy to make and keeps really well in the fridge.

- **16-oz. pkg. coleslaw mix**
- **1/3 c. salted cocktail peanuts**
- **1/3 c. raisins**
- **1/2 c. mayonnaise**
- **1 T. red wine vinegar**
- **1 t. sugar**

Combine slaw mix, peanuts and raisins in a large bowl; set aside. In a separate small bowl, combine mayonnaise, vinegar and sugar; stir until well blended. Fold mayonnaise mixture into slaw and combine well. Cover and refrigerate at least one hour before serving.

Serves 6 to 8

WORLD-FAMOUS GREEN BEANS

INGRID SHEWMAKE
JOPLIN, MO

My mother-in-law has always treated me like her own daughter and been a great teacher to me in the art of cooking. This simple recipe has started my husband bragging on my cooking many a time... when actually I got the secret from his mom!

- **4 15-oz. cans green beans**
- **6 to 8 cubes beef bouillon**
- **1/2 c. butter, sliced**
- **1/2 c. onion, finely chopped**
- **pepper to taste**
- **Optional: 1/2 c. bacon bits**

Combine all ingredients in a medium saucepan over medium heat. Bring to a rolling boil; reduce heat to medium-low and simmer for 20 to 30 minutes.

Serves 6

FROSTY WALDORF SALAD

SUSAN BICK
BALLWIN, MO

A fruity favorite at all of our family gatherings.

- 1/2 c. sugar
- 1/2 c. pineapple juice
- 1/4 c. lemon juice
- 1/8 t. salt
- 1/4 c. celery, diced
- 1/2 c. mini marshmallows
- 1/2 c. seedless red grapes, halved
- 1/4 c. diced pears, drained
- 1/2 c. crushed pineapple, drained
- 2 apples, cored and diced
- 1/4 c. chopped walnuts
- 1/4 c. chopped pecans
- 1-1/3 c. whipping cream

Combine sugar, juices and salt in a large saucepan. Cook over medium heat, stirring often, until thickened. Remove from heat; let cool completely. Stir in celery, marshmallows, fruit and nuts. In a chilled bowl with an electric mixer on medium speed, whip cream until soft peaks form; fold into fruit mixture. Spoon into an ungreased 8"x8" baking pan; freeze. Remove from freezer 5 minutes before serving. Cut into squares to serve.

Serves 9

PRESENTATION

Simple garnishes dress up main dishes all year 'round! Fresh mint sprigs add coolness and color to summertime dishes, while rosemary sprigs and cranberries add a festive touch to holiday platters.

BAKED SPINACH SUPREME

KATHIE MOSS
SAINT LOUIS, MO

Delicious...even spinach haters like it!

- **10-oz. pkg. frozen chopped spinach, thawed and drained**
- **1 T. onion, minced**
- **1/2 c. tomato sauce**
- **1 c. shredded Cheddar cheese**
- **1 c. sour cream**
- **4-oz. can mushroom stems and pieces, drained**

Combine all ingredients; transfer to a greased 2-quart casserole dish. Bake, uncovered, at 350 degrees for 30 to 40 minutes, until hot and bubbly.

Serves 4 to 6

CORN & BROCCOLI CASSEROLE

MARIAN FORCK
CHAMOIS, MO

This simple recipe is so flavorful. Better make a double batch...it's sure to be a hit!

- **15-oz. pkg. frozen chopped broccoli, cooked and well drained**
- **14-3/4 oz. can cream-style corn**
- **1 egg, beaten**
- **1 t. dried, chopped onion**
- **12 round buttery crackers, crushed**
- **1/4 c. butter, melted**

In a bowl, combine broccoli, corn, egg and onion. Spray a 9"x9" baking pan with non-stick vegetable spray; spread mixture in pan. Toss cracker crumbs with melted butter; sprinkle over broccoli mixture. Bake, uncovered, at 350 degrees for 30 minutes, or until golden and heated through.

Serves 6

PATTY'S AU GRATIN POTATOES

PATTY HART
EUGENE, MO

I'm sharing this recipe in memory of my niece Lindsey. It was her very favorite and she always asked me to bring it to family get-togethers.

- **32-oz. pkg. frozen shredded hashbrowns**
- **2 12-oz. containers sour cream**
- **2 10-3/4 oz. cans cream of mushroom soup**
- **1/4 c. milk**
- **chopped onion to taste**
- **seasoned salt and pepper to taste**
- **6 to 9 slices American cheese**
- **1/2 c. butter, sliced**

Combine all ingredients except cheese and butter in a large bowl. Mix well. In a slow cooker, alternate layers of the hashbrown mixture and cheese, beginning and ending with the hashbrowns. Top with butter. Cover and cook on high setting for 1-1/2 hours; turn to low, cook 2-1/2 hours longer, or until potatoes are tender.

Serves 8 to 10

MOM'S OYSTER DRESSING

LEEANN EDWARDS
BILLINGS, MO

For several years Mom made this dish for our family Thanksgiving and Christmas dinners. My dad and brothers still request it every year so now I make it. It doesn't taste quite the same as Mom's, but it's close!

- **14-3/4 oz. can creamed corn**
- **8-oz. can smoked oysters, drained**
- **1/2 c. evaporated milk**
- **1/2 c. butter, softened**
- **1 sleeve saltine crackers, crumbled**

In a lightly greased 12"x8" baking pan, mix all ingredients in order given. Add more crackers if a thicker consistency is desired. Bake, uncovered, at 350 degrees for 35 to 40 minutes.

Serves 4

BARLEY & SWEET CORN BAKE

JULIE FRANCIS
CAPE GIRARDEAU, MO

This hearty, colorful casserole goes well with pork, chicken or fish. For convenience, it can be made ahead and refrigerated.

3 cloves garlic, minced
1 c. onion, chopped
2/3 c. carrots, peeled and chopped
1 T. oil
3 c. chicken broth
1 c. pearled barley, uncooked
Optional: 1/4 t. salt
1/8 t. pepper
2 c. frozen corn, thawed
1/2 c. fresh parsley, chopped

In a skillet over medium heat, sauté garlic, onion and carrots in oil until tender. Transfer to a greased 2-quart casserole dish; add broth, barley, salt if desired and pepper. Mix well. Cover and bake at 350 degrees for one hour. Stir in corn and parsley. Cover and bake an additional 10 to 15 minutes, or until barley is tender and corn is heated through.

Serves 10 to 12

DINNERTIME CONVERSATION

Saint Louis hosted the 1904 Summer Olympics... the first Olympic Games ever held in the U.S... at the same time as the World's Fair. It was complete chaos. Athletes competed for four and a half months with one event each day of the fair. But only 42 of the 91 events actually included competitors from other countries. Almost half of the runners got heat stroke, and the first-place winner cheated by hitching a car ride from mile nine to mile 19.

SCRUMPTIOUS SPINACH PIE

BECKY HALL
BELTON, MO

If you can't make the farmers' market Saturday, don't fret...a 10-ounce bag of baby spinach from your local grocer equals 6 cups fresh spinach.

6 c. baby spinach, trimmed

1/4 c. onion, chopped
2 eggs, beaten
2 T. grated Parmesan cheese
1 c. milk
1/3 c. celery, chopped
1/2 t. salt
1/2 t. nutmeg

Rinse spinach, chop and place in a large saucepan over high heat. Cook, covered, 5 minutes, or until wilted. Drain, pressing out as much liquid as possible. Combine remaining ingredients; fold into spinach. Spoon mixture into a well-greased 9" pie plate. Bake at 375 degrees for 45 minutes, or until a knife inserted near the middle comes out clean. Cut into 6 wedges and serve warm.

Serves 6

SWEET POTATO MEDALLIONS

ANITA MULLINS
ELDRIDGE, MO

My husband loves sweet potato casserole for holiday dinners, so I came up with this easier version using his favorite ingredients from the casserole... brown sugar and pecans.

4 sweet potatoes
1/4 c. butter
3/4 to 1 c. dark brown sugar, packed
1/2 c. chopped pecans

Cover potatoes with water in a large saucepan. Bring to a boil over heat; cook until tender but not soft. Drain and let cool; pull off peels. Slice into 1/2 to 1-inch medallions; set aside. Melt butter in a large skillet over medium heat. Add sweet potato medallions; sprinkle with brown sugar and divide pecans evenly among medallions. Simmer until brown sugar dissolves and sweet potatoes are heated through and fork-tender.

Serves 4

FARMHOUSE EGG NOODLES

ANGELA MILLER
JEFFERSON CITY, MO

These scrumptious homemade noodles have been a tradition in our family for many years. Unrolling the noodles has always been the children's job...they love helping out!

1 c. all-purpose flour
1 egg, beaten
3 T. milk
1/8 t. salt
3 to 4 14-1/2 oz. cans chicken broth

Place flour in a large bowl; make a well in the center and add egg, milk and salt. Slowly stir to mix in flour until a soft ball forms; knead in any remaining flour. Roll out dough on a floured surface to about 1/4-inch thick. Roll up dough jelly-roll style; slice across to cut noodles about 1/2-inch wide. Unroll noodles and pile them on a floured surface while waiting for broth to warm. In a large saucepan, bring broth to a boil. Drop noodles into broth. Cook until tender, about 8 to 10 minutes.

Serves 4 to 6

MOOSE'S GARDEN SALAD

PATTI BARNETT
HILLSBORO, MO

My husband wanted to try something different after harvesting bushels of fresh tomatoes and cukes from the garden...this zesty tasting salad was the result.

Combine tomatoes, cucumber and onion in a serving bowl; sprinkle with salt and pepper to taste. Add cheese, olives and salad dressing; toss well. Serve immediately, or refrigerate up to 2 days.

Serves 6

2 tomatoes, diced
1 cucumber, peeled and diced
1/2 onion, diced
salt and pepper to taste
1/2 c. crumbled feta cheese
2-1/4 oz. can sliced black olives, drained
2 T. Greek salad dressing

SWEET-AND-SOUR GREEN BEANS

PAULA JAMES
EDGAR SPRINGS, MO

This recipe was originally my sister's, and it's one of my favorites. Everyone I have made these beans for loves them...I often get calls from family & friends wanting the recipe.

In a deep skillet over medium heat, cook bacon until crisp; drain. Drain half the liquid from beans; add beans to skillet. Stir in remaining ingredients. Simmer over low heat for about 45 minutes, until some of the liquid has evaporated.

Serves 6 to 8

4 slices bacon, cut into 1-inch pieces
2 14-1/2 oz. cans cut green beans
1/2 c. onion, chopped
1/3 c. brown sugar, packed
1/3 c. vinegar
salt and pepper to taste

ITALIAN ZUCCHINI

STEPHANIE GEGG
SAINTE GENEVIEVE, MO

I love summer gardening and all my fresh produce! This makes a great side dish at any barbecue. I've even enjoyed it as my main dish...it's a satisfying meatless meal.

1-1/2 c. zucchini, cubed
15-1/2 oz. can petite diced tomatoes
1 c. sweet onion, chopped
1 c. sliced mushrooms
1/2 t. garlic, minced
1/2 t. red pepper flakes
1/8 t. dried oregano
1/2 t. salt
1/8 t. pepper

Combine zucchini, undrained tomatoes and remaining ingredients in a medium saucepan. Cook over medium heat for 20 to 25 minutes, until vegetables are tender.

Serves 4

FAVORITE STIR-FRIED ZUCCHINI

MARSHA POUNDS
ROLLA, MO

Our garden produces lots of zucchini, and this is one of my favorite recipes for preparing it. It has been updated from a mid-1970s cookbook. My husband and I are trying to eat more a heart-healthy diet, so I decreased the amounts of fat and salt in the recipe.

1 T. olive oil
1 lb. zucchini, cut lengthwise into strips
1 onion, thinly sliced
1 T. sesame seed
1 T. soy sauce
1/4 t. sea salt

Heat oil in a large skillet over medium heat; add zucchini and onion. Cook for 5 to 10 minutes, stirring frequently, until crisp-tender. Quickly stir in sesame seed, soy sauce and salt. Heat through and serve promptly.

Serves 4

TEXAS COWBOY BEANS

SARA JANE INMAN
POMONA, MO

These beans are practically a meal in themselves! A big pan of cornbread and a tall glass of iced tea are all you need to make them into a quick & easy dinner.

- **1-1/2 lbs. ground beef**
- **8 slices bacon, chopped**
- **1 onion, chopped**
- **16-oz. can butter beans**
- **15-oz. can pork and beans**
- **16-oz. can pinto beans**
- **16-oz. can kidney beans**
- **1/4 c. catsup**
- **2 t. mustard**
- **1/4 c. barbecue sauce**
- **2 T. light corn syrup**
- **1/3 c. brown sugar, packed**
- **1 t. chili powder**
- **1 t. salt**
- **1 t. Pepper**

Brown beef in a skillet over medium heat; drain. Combine beef, bacon, undrained beans and remaining ingredients in a lightly greased 13"x9" baking pan; stir to mix well. Bake, uncovered, at 350 degrees for 45 minutes. Let stand for 5 minutes to thicken before serving.

Serves 10 to 12

KITCHEN TIP

A melon baller has lots of uses besides making juicy fruit salads. Put it to work forming perfect balls of cookie dough, coring apples and even making pretty little servings of butter for the dinner table. Clever!

PASTA CON BROCCOLI

LISA PAYNE
SAINT LOUIS, MO

I love this recipe...it tastes amazing and can be prepared in about 30 minutes! I made some adjustments to cut the fat, and my family can't even tell the difference. Sometimes I stir in some diced grilled chicken to make it heartier.

8-oz. pkg. medium shell pasta, uncooked
1/4 c. butter, sliced
1 c. regular half-and-half
1 c. fat-free half-and-half
1/4 c. tomato sauce
1 t. garlic powder
12-oz. pkg. frozen broccoli flowerets in steamer bag
1 t. salt
pepper to taste
1/2 c. grated Parmesan cheese

Cook pasta according to package directions for half the time given, about 5 minutes. Drain; return to cooking pot. Stir in butter, half-and-half, tomato sauce and garlic powder; bring to a boil. Meanwhile, microwave broccoli according to package directions; drain. When pasta is just tender, stir in broccoli, salt and pepper. Remove from heat; stir in Parmesan cheese.

Serves 4

FROZEN FRUIT CUPS

TERESA POTTER
BRANSON, MO

A friend gave me this recipe after serving it at a ladies' tea. It's a really easy make-ahead recipe...no last-minute fuss!

16-oz. can fruit cocktail
2 to 3 bananas, sliced
1 t. lemon juice
2/3 c. mayonnaise
8-oz. container frozen whipped topping, thawed
Garnish: maraschino cherries

In a bowl, combine undrained fruit cocktail, bananas and lemon juice. Stir in mayonnaise and whipped topping. Spoon mixture into 12 paper-lined muffin cups; top each with a cherry. Place muffin tin in freezer. Once frozen, individual cups may be placed in plastic freezer bags and stored in the freezer for several weeks. To serve, arrange on a serving tray and let stand at room temperature 10 to 15 minutes.

Serves 12

HEARTY SQUASH CASSEROLE

SARINA SKIDMORE
SPRINGFIELD, MO

A family favorite on chilly evenings...super for potlucks too.

1 c. yellow squash, shredded
2 potatoes, peeled and sliced
1/3 c. red onion, chopped
14-1/2 oz. can diced tomatoes with basil, garlic & oregano, drained
1/2 c. butter, melted
8-oz. pkg. chicken-flavored stuffing mix
1-1/2 lbs. ground beef, browned and drained
2 10-3/4 oz. cans cream of mushroom soup
1-1/3 c. water

Lightly spray a 3-1/2 quart casserole dish with non-stick vegetable spray. Layer squash, potatoes, onion and tomatoes in dish; set aside. In a separate bowl, toss together melted butter and stuffing. Spoon over tomatoes. In another bowl, mix ground beef, soups and water; spoon over stuffing mixture. Cover and bake at 350 degrees for one hour, or until bubbly and vegetables are tender.

Serves 6 to 8

MOM'S GREEN BEANS & BACON

CINDY DECARLO
SULLIVAN, MO

My mother always simmered these green beans all day on the stovetop. I've turned it into an easy slow-cooker recipe...it's still the most scrumptious way to enjoy green beans!

- **4 14-1/2 oz. cans green beans, drained**
- **2 14-oz. cans chicken broth with roasted garlic**
- **1 onion, cut into 6 wedges**
- **1/2 lb. bacon, diced and partially cooked, drippings reserved**
- **salt and pepper to taste**

Place all ingredients in a slow cooker; stir. Cover and cook on low setting for 8 hours, or on high setting for 5 hours.

Serves 6

GOLDEN PARMESAN ROASTED POTATOES

LINDA HENDRIX
MOUNDVILLE, MO

Pop into the oven alongside a roast for a homestyle dinner that can't be beat.

- **1/4 c. all-purpose flour**
- **1/4 c. grated Parmesan cheese**
- **3/4 t. salt**
- **1/8 t. pepper**
- **6 potatoes, peeled and cut into wedges**
- **1/3 c. butter, melted**
- **Garnish: fresh parsley, chopped**

Place flour, cheese, salt and pepper in a large plastic zipping bag; mix well. Add potato wedges; shake to coat. Pour butter into a 13"x9" baking pan, tilting to coat; arrange potatoes in pan. Bake, uncovered, at 375 degrees for one hour. Sprinkle with parsley.

Serves 4 to 6

WHITE BEAN SALAD

AMY GROUNSELL
KANSAS CITY, MO

I discovered this recipe in my local paper, and it's since become a family favorite. Sun-dried tomato-infused oil is easier to find than you'd think...just pour it right from the jar of sun-dried tomatoes!

- **1/4 c. extra-virgin olive oil**
- **2 T. sun-dried tomato-infused oil**
- **1/4 c. sun-dried tomatoes, chopped**
- **1 T. red wine vinegar**
- **1/4 t. salt**
- **1/4 t. pepper**
- **2 16-oz. cans cannellini beans, drained and rinsed**
- **1/3 c. red onion, diced**
- **2 cloves garlic, minced**
- **6 leaves basil, thinly sliced**
- **1/4 c. grated Romano cheese**

In a small bowl, combine olive oil, tomato oil, sun-dried tomatoes, vinegar, salt and pepper. Place beans in a serving bowl; pour oil mixture over top. Cover; chill for one hour. Toss; sprinkle with remaining ingredients. Serve immediately.

Serves 6 to 8

JUST FOR FUN

Richland, Missouri, is the only city in the U.S. with a cave restaurant.

WANDA & VICKIE'S BAKED BEANS

WANDA SIDEBOTTOM
LAKE OZARK, MO

When I was in trade school, one of the students brought in this recipe to share with everyone. My late daughter, Vickie, and I used to serve this recipe at all kinds of parties.

- **1 lb. brown & serve pork sausage links, cut into bite-size pieces**
- **1 green pepper, chopped**
- **1 onion, chopped**
- **2 28-oz. cans pork & beans**
- **1 c. catsup**
- **1/4 c. brown sugar, packed**
- **2 T. Worcestershire sauce**
- **1 T. smoke-flavored cooking sauce**
- **1/2 to 1 t. hot pepper sauce**

In a skillet over medium-high heat, brown sausage links. Drain; add green pepper and onion. Reduce heat to low; cook until onion is translucent, about 2 minutes. Transfer to a 13"x9" baking pan sprayed lightly with non-stick vegetable spray. Add remaining ingredients and mix well; cover with aluminum foil. Bake at 375 degrees for 45 minutes to one hour.

Serves 6 to 8

VEGGIE TRIO SALAD

LINDA MYERS
DENVER, MO

There were gardens galore this year, and everyone had bumper crops. I've had a large amount of yellow squash, one neighbor had cherry tomatoes and yet another neighbor red onions. We all shared our harvest, and I decided to use just these three in a recipe.

- **2 c. cherry tomatoes, halved**
- **1 red onion, halved and sliced**
- **1 to 2 yellow squash, peeled and cut into 1-inch cubes**
- **2 T. balsamic vinegar**
- **2 T. extra-virgin olive oil**
- **1/4 t. salt**
- **1/4 t. pepper**

Combine vegetables in a large serving bowl and toss with a spoon. Whisk together vinegar, oil, salt and pepper. Pour over vegetables and stir well to coat. Serve immediately, or cover and chill.

Serves 4 to 6

MEXICAN HOMINY

MARY STEPHENSON
GROVESPRING, MO

A side dish for your favorite Mexican dinner that's just a bit different! Make it milder or hotter simply by using different chiles.

- **2 15-1/2 oz. cans yellow hominy, drained**
- **2 15-1/2 oz. cans white hominy, drained**
- **4-oz. can chopped green chiles**
- **8-oz. container sour cream**
- **1 c. shredded Colby cheese**
- **1/2 t. onion powder**
- **1/4 t. garlic powder**
- **salt to taste**

Combine all ingredients in a greased slow cooker. Cover and cook on low setting for 2 to 3 hours, until hot and bubbly.

Serves 8

SWEETIE'S DRESSING

PATRICIA BUCHANAN
COLUMBIA, MO

Everyone called Mom "Sweetie" which she certainly was. There are a lot of great cooks, but our Sweetie was the best. She didn't use a recipe very often...she just made it up as she went. This is our best rendition of her delicious dressing that we enjoyed every holiday.

1/2 c. onion, chopped
1/2 c. celery, chopped
1 to 2 T. butter
1-1/2 loaves white bread, cubed and dried
3 14-oz. cans chicken broth
10-3/4 oz. can cream of celery soup
4 eggs, beaten
2 t. dried sage
1 t. dried parsley
salt and pepper to taste

In a skillet over medium heat, sauté onion and celery in butter. Transfer onion mixture to a very large bowl; add remaining ingredients and toss to mix. Spread in a lightly greased 13"x9" baking pan. Bake, uncovered, at 375 degrees for one hour and 15 minutes.

Serves 10 to 12

DALE'S RICE DISH

MELISSA SCOTT
O'FALLON, MO

This recipe is perfect for the family get-togethers. It's been a favorite of my daughter for 16 years.

4 c. instant rice, uncooked
1 lb. bacon
1 bunch green onions, diced
7-oz. can mushroom stems & pieces, drained
soy sauce to taste

Prepare rice according to package directions. Meanwhile, cook bacon in a skillet over medium heat until crisp. Drain and chop bacon; reserve some drippings in pan. Stir onions and mushrooms into drippings; simmer until tender. Add cooked rice and bacon to skillet. Stir in enough soy sauce to turn mixture brown. Simmer until heated through.

Serves 8 to 10

CHAPTER THREE

Show-Me Soups & Sandwiches

GATHER 'ROUND THE CAMPFIRE TOGETHER WITH FAMILY & FRIENDS TO COZY UP WITH A BOWL OF HEARTY SOUP OR A TASTY SANDWICH PERFECT FOR PACK'N IN THE SADDLE BAG!

COWBOY STEW

SUE ELLEN MORRISON
BLUE SPRING, MO

This is one of my family's favorite meals. It is wonderful with cornbread or hushpuppies, even plain old crackers. This will fill up a hungry family and it can simmer while you work or play.

- **1 lb. ground beef**
- **1/2 c. onion, finely chopped**
- **salt and pepper to taste**
- **8-oz. can tomato sauce**
- **2 15-oz. cans ranch-style beans or chili beans**
- **15-oz. can sweet corn and diced peppers, drained**
- **1 baking potato, peeled and cubed**

In a skillet over medium heat, brown beef and onion; drain. Season beef mixture with salt and pepper; transfer to a slow cooker. Pour tomato sauce over top. Add beans, corn, potato and just enough water to cover ingredients. Stir gently to mix. Cover and cook on low setting for 2 hours, or until potato is tender.

Serves 4 to 6

PULLED BBQ CHICKEN

JENITA DAVISON
LA PLATA, MO

Saucy and yummy on a bun! Serve with potato chips or a tossed green salad.

- **6 boneless, skinless chicken breasts**
- **18-oz. bottle sweet onion barbecue sauce, or other favorite sauce**
- **1/2 c. Italian salad dressing**
- **1/4 c. light brown sugar, packed**
- **2 T. Worcestershire sauce**
- **sandwich buns, split**

Place chicken in a slow cooker. Combine remaining ingredients except buns; spoon over chicken. Cover and cook on low setting for 6 to 8 hours, or on high setting for 3 to 4 hours. Using 2 forks, shred chicken in the sauce; stir. Serve chicken mixture spooned onto buns.

Serves 6

CREAMY CHICKEN-RICE SOUP

AMANDA HETTINGER
KIRKWOOD, MO

I make this hearty soup on Christmas Eve to enjoy with crusty rolls while watching our favorite Christmas movie. A deli roast chicken makes it simple and delicious. When I think of this soup, I think of comfort and joyful memories...it really is a wonderful life!

8 c. chicken broth
1/2 c. onion, finely chopped
1 cube chicken bouillon
1/4 t. garlic powder
1/4 t. dried thyme
1/4 c. butter, sliced
1/4 c. all-purpose flour
10-3/4 oz. can low-sodium cream of chicken soup
1/2 c. white wine or chicken broth
3 c. cooked chicken breast, shredded
4 c. cooked wild rice

Combine broth, onion, bouillon and seasonings in a soup pot over high heat. Bring to a boil; reduce heat to medium-low and simmer for 30 minutes. In another large soup pot, melt butter over medium heat. Whisk in flour until smooth; cook for 2 to 3 minutes, until mixture loses its flour taste. Gradually whisk in hot broth mixture. Bring to a boil; cook and stir for 2 minutes, or until slightly thickened. Whisk in canned soup and wine or broth. Stir in chicken and cooked rice; heat through.

Serves 8

HOMEMADE CHICKEN NOODLE SOUP

MICHELLE KISER
NIXA, MO

This is one of my family's most-requested wintertime meals. It not only warms them up, but fills the house with a delicious smell!

- **16-oz. pkg. frozen egg noodles, uncooked**
- **1 c. carrot, peeled and chopped**
- **1/2 c. onion, chopped**
- **1/2 c. celery, chopped**
- **5 cubes chicken bouillon**
- **3 bay leaves**
- **1 t. garlic powder**
- **1/2 t. dried thyme**
- **salt and pepper to taste**
- **3 chicken breasts, cooked and shredded**
- **1 c. milk**
- **1/2 c. frozen peas**
- **Garnish: shredded cheese, saltine crackers**

Cook noodles according to package directions; drain. Meanwhile, in a separate stockpot, combine carrot, onion and celery. Barely cover with water. Add bouillon cubes and seasonings. Bring to a boil over medium-high heat. Reduce heat to low; simmer until vegetables are tender, about 15 minutes. Do not drain. Add chicken, cooked egg noodles and enough water to cover all ingredients. Bring water back to a boil; reduce heat to low. Simmer for about 30 minutes, stirring occasionally. Add milk and frozen peas during the last 5 to 10 minutes. Remove bay leaves before serving. Serve with shredded cheese and crackers.

Serves 12

ROAST CHICKEN-CORN TORTILLA SOUP

SHERRY NOBLE
KENNETT, MO

Garnish with quick-fried strips of red corn tortillas.

- 1 deli roast chicken, cut into bite-size pieces
- 4 c. chicken broth
- 1/2 c. chipotle salsa
- 1/2 c. tequila lime salsa
- 1 to 2 c. corn tortilla chips, crushed
- juice of 1/2 lime
- 1/2 c. fresh cilantro, chopped
- salt and pepper
- Optional: shredded Cheddar cheese, sour cream

Combine chicken, broth and salsas in a large saucepan over medium-high heat. Add tortilla chips and simmer for 10 minutes. Stir in lime juice, cilantro, salt and pepper. Serve immediately, garnished with cheese and sour cream, if desired.

Serves 4

DINNERTIME CONVERSATION

Kansas City, Missouri has more fountains than any other city in the world except Rome. Hence Kansas City is known as the City of Fountains.

SWEET POTATO-CORN CHOWDER

GAIL WRIGHT
BELLFLOWER, MO

This is a very tasty chowder that I love to make in the fall and winter. It's ready to serve in about an hour.

- 14-oz. pkg. Kielbasa sausage ring, diced
- 1 c. onion, chopped
- 1 T. garlic, minced
- 3 T. all-purpose flour
- 1-1/2 t. ground cumin
- 1-1/2 t. chili powder
- 6 c. chicken broth
- 16-oz. pkg. frozen corn
- 2 c. sweet potatoes, peeled and cubed
- 3/4 lb. boneless, skinless, chicken breasts, chopped
- 1 c. whipping cream
- 1 t. pepper

In a Dutch oven over medium heat, brown sausage for 5 minutes, stirring occasionally. Add onion and garlic. Cook and stir for 5 minutes. Stir in flour, cumin and chili powder. Cook and stir for 2 minutes longer. Stir in chicken broth; bring to a boil. Add corn, sweet potatoes and chicken; return to a boil. Reduce heat and simmer, covered, for about 20 minutes, or until sweet potatoes are tender and chicken is cooked through. Stir in cream and pepper; heat through.

Serves 8 to 10

JUST FOR FUN

In 1873, Susan Elizabeth Blow opened the first public kindergarten in the United States in Saint Louis.

CARLA'S NOT REALLY CHILI

CARLA STRICKLIN
VALLEY PARK, MO

When we were expecting a snowstorm, I picked up the essentials at the grocery, thinking I had the ingredients for chili on hand. But, that evening after the snow started in earnest, I realized I was mistaken in that assumption. So, I put this mixture of ingredients into the slow cooker, and it turned out to be quite a hit!

1 lb. lean ground beef, browned and drained
16-oz. can black beans, drained and rinsed
10-oz. can diced tomatoes with green chiles
15-1/4 oz. can corn, drained
2 to 4 T. taco seasoning mix
salt and pepper to taste
1 to 2 c. cocktail vegetable juice to taste
Garnish: sour cream, shredded Cheddar cheese, salsa, chopped green onions

Combine all ingredients except juice and garnish in a slow cooker; stir to blend. Pour in juice until mixture is of desired consistency. Cover and cook at high setting for one to 1-1/2 hours. Reduce to low setting and cook for an additional 30 minutes. Garnish as desired.

Serves 4 to 6

CREAMY GARDEN CHOWDER

SHARON CRIDER
JUNCTION CITY, MO

This cheesy soup is so satisfying! It's a tasty way to use up all those odds & ends in the fridge too. Just substitute 2 cups cooked, chopped veggies for the package of frozen vegetables.

10-oz. pkg. frozen mixed vegetables, cooked and drained
10-3/4 oz. can cream of chicken soup
1-1/4 c. milk
Garnish: 1 c. shredded Cheddar cheese

Combine vegetables, soup and milk in a saucepan over medium-low heat. Heat to simmering, stirring occasionally. Sprinkle with cheese before serving.

Serves 4

ANITA'S CORNED BEEF SOUP

ANITA MULLINS
ELDRIDGE, MO

When I was single and living on my own, I loved corned beef hash and corned beef & cabbage, but neither was very tasty reheated as leftovers. So I combined the two to make a big pot of yummy soup that I could reheat and eat for days...the flavor just gets better! Now that I'm married, my family loves this soup too.

1 head cabbage, chopped
4 to 5 potatoes, peeled and diced
1 onion, diced
Optional: 1 to 2 carrots, peeled and sliced
3 cubes beef bouillon
2 cubes chicken bouillon
salt and pepper to taste
12-oz. can corned beef, cubed

In a Dutch oven over medium heat, combine all ingredients except corned beef. Cover with water; cook for about 15 minutes, until vegetables are almost tender. Stir in corned beef; add more salt or pepper, if desired. Continue cooking until vegetables are tender.

Serves 4 to 6

GARLICKY GREEN CHILI

TAMMY BURNETT
SPRINGFIELD, MO

My boss gave me this recipe, and I've found that every time I prepare it, guests ask me for the recipe!

- **3 lbs. boneless pork chops, cubed**
- **2 T. oil**
- **1/4 c. all-purpose flour**
- **2 T. garlic, minced**
- **salt and pepper to taste**
- **2 4-oz. cans diced green chiles**
- **14-1/2 oz. can chicken broth**
- **16-oz. jar chunky salsa**
- **1 bunch fresh cilantro, chopped**
- **1 t. ground cumin**

In a Dutch oven over medium heat, brown pork in oil. Mix in flour; stir for one minute. Add garlic, salt and pepper, cook for 2 minutes. Stir in remaining ingredients; simmer for 45 minutes.

Serves 8

GRILLED SALAMI PIZZA SANDWICHES

SHARON CRIDER
JUNCTION CITY, KS

A family favorite for years!

- **2/3 c. pizza sauce**
- **8 slices bread**
- **4 slices deli salami**
- **4 slices American cheese**
- **garlic salt to taste**
- **butter to taste, softened**

Spread pizza sauce on one side of 4 bread slices. Top each bread slice with one salami slice and one cheese slice; sprinkle with garlic salt. Top with remaining bread slices. Generously butter top and bottom of sandwiches. Heat a skillet over medium heat; add sandwiches and cook on both sides until bread is toasted and cheese is melted

Makes 4 sandwiches.

BONNIE'S CHICKEN NOODLE SOUP

SHARON ALEXANDER
INDEPENDENCE, MO

This is my mom's recipe...she's an awesome cook! She loves to cook for people, to help them in time of need or just to bless them for no special reason at all. I've fixed this soup for co-workers, friends at church and other family members, and everyone raves about how delicious it is. So to honor her and her giving spirit, I wanted to share this recipe for everyone to enjoy.

3 boneless, skinless chicken breasts
chicken & poultry seasoning to taste
3 10-1/2 oz. cans chicken broth
4 c. water
2 cubes chicken bouillon
1/2 t. curry powder
1 t. garlic salt, or more to taste
10 baby carrots, chopped
1/4 c. onion, chopped
1 stalk celery, chopped
12-oz. pkg. extra broad no-yolk noodles, uncooked
3 10-3/4 oz. cans cream of chicken soup

Season chicken lightly on all sides with chicken seasoning. Arrange chicken in a lightly greased 13"x9" baking pan. Bake, uncovered, at 400 degrees for 20 to 25 minutes, until chicken juices run clear; set aside to cool. Meanwhile, combine chicken broth, water and bouillon cubes in a large soup pot. Bring to a boil over high heat; season with curry powder and garlic salt. Reduce heat to medium. Add vegetables; simmer until partially tender. Add noodles; cook until tender. Dice baked chicken and add to broth. Stir in chicken soup; add more water to desired consistency, if too thick. Simmer for a few more minutes.

Serves 8 to 10

CHEDDAR-HAM CHOWDER

LORI BRODERICK
PLATTSBURG, MO

A friend gave me this recipe, and the first time I made it for my family, they licked the pan clean. No leftovers! Since then, I double the recipe when I make it, because it makes a great lunch too.

- **2 c. water**
- **2 c. potatoes, peeled and cubed**
- **1/2 c. celery, sliced**
- **1/2 c. carrots, peeled and sliced**
- **1/2 c. onion, chopped**
- **1 t. salt**
- **1/2 t. pepper**
- **1/4 c. butter**
- **1/4 c. all-purpose flour**
- **2 c. milk**
- **8-oz. container shredded sharp Cheddar cheese**
- **15-1/4 oz. can corn**
- **1-1/2 c. cooked ham, cubed**

In a large saucepan over medium-high heat, bring water to a boil. Add potatoes, celery, carrots, onion, salt and pepper. Reduce heat to medium-low. Cover and simmer for 8 to 10 minutes, just until vegetables are tender. Remove from heat; do not drain. Meanwhile, in a medium saucepan over medium heat, melt butter. Blend in flour; add milk all at once. Cook and stir until thickened and bubbly. Add cheese; stir until melted. Add milk mixture to vegetable mixture in large saucepan; stir well. Add corn and ham. Heat through over medium heat, stirring occasionally.

Serves 4

ASIAN-INSPIRED SHORT RIB SOUP

PENNY SHERMAN
AVA, MO

A new Asian restaurant opened up in town, and I tried a dish very similar to this one. I love the slightly spicy flavor of this soup. This is my effort to recreate it at home...a pretty good interpretation, I'd say!

6 lbs. beef short ribs, cut into serving-size pieces
4 c. low-sodium chicken broth
1/3 c. soy sauce
1/4 c. sugar
3 T. fresh ginger, peeled and grated
2 T. sriracha hot chili sauce
2 T. toasted sesame oil
4 cloves garlic, finely chopped
1 bunch green onions
12-oz. pkg. rice noodles, uncooked
Garnish: grated carrot, sliced cucumber, chopped fresh cilantro, lime wedges

Place ribs in a large slow cooker; set aside. In a bowl, whisk together broth, soy sauce, sugar, ginger, chili sauce, oil and garlic. Thinly slice white part of onions and stir into broth mixture. Spoon broth mixture over ribs. Cover and cook on high setting for 6 hours, until ribs are very tender. About 30 minutes before serving, prepare noodles according to package directions. Drain; divide noodles evenly among 6 bowls. Skim fat from soup in slow cooker; ladle broth and ribs over noodles. Garnish servings as desired.

Serves 6 to 8

HEARTY ITALIAN CHILI

MOLLY CARTER
POWERSVILLE, MO

I started making this chili when my husband and I were dating. With a couple of minor tweaks, it soon became one of his favorites.

1 lb. ground beef
1/2 lb. ground Italian pork sausage
1 onion, chopped
1/2 c. green pepper, chopped
14-1/2 oz. can diced tomatoes
26-oz. jar spaghetti sauce
1 c. water
16-oz. can kidney beans, drained and rinsed
14-1/2 oz. can sliced mushrooms, drained
1/3 c. pepperoni slices, halved
1 t. chili powder
1/2 t. salt
1/8 t. Pepper

In a large saucepan over medium heat, cook beef, sausage, onion and green pepper until meats are no longer pink; drain. Stir in tomatoes with juice and remaining ingredients; bring to a boil. Reduce heat to low. Simmer, uncovered, for 30 minutes, stirring occasionally.

Makes 6 to 8 servings

PRESENTATION

Set up a framed menu to let everyone know that delicious dishes like Great Grandmother's Pot Roast and Aunt Betty's Pudding Cake await!

EASY BUT ELEGANT CHICKEN SALAD

ANITA MULLINS
ELDRIDGE, MO

This is a last-minute recipe I came up with for my granddaughter's birthday. I stopped to pick up canned chicken, then tossed it together and made finger sandwiches. It was a huge hit and was requested for another grandchild's birthday a few weeks later! No matter how much I make, I never have leftovers.

2 to 3 6-oz. cans chicken, drained and flaked
1/4 c. sweetened dried cranberries, chopped
1 stalk celery, finely chopped
1/4 c. pecans, finely minced
1 c. mayonnaise, or to taste
Optional: bread, lettuce leaves

Combine all ingredients except bread or lettuce in a bowl; mix well. For the best flavor, cover and refrigerate overnight before serving. Spread on bread for finger sandwiches, or serve on lettuce leaves as a salad.

Serves 4 to 6

DINNERTIME CONVERSATION

Eight different states border Missouri, making it one of two states with the highest number of neighboring states. Tennessee also has eight bordering states.

TURKEY NOODLE SOUP

ERIN KELLY
JEFFERSON CITY, MO

My mom and I first made this recipe for dinner after going to a fall festival. It was a warm and delicious end to a great day with her, and a good way to use up leftover turkey!

- **5 c. chicken broth**
- **10-3/4 oz. can cream of chicken soup**
- **15-oz. can corn, drained**
- **salt and pepper to taste**
- **1/2 c. onion, finely chopped**
- **1/2 c. green onions, sliced**
- **1/2 c. carrot, peeled and finely chopped**
- **1/2 c. celery, finely chopped**
- **1-1/2 c. medium egg noodles, uncooked**
- **2 c. cooked turkey, chopped**

In a slow cooker, combine all ingredients except noodles and turkey. Cover and cook on low setting for 4 to 5 hours. Stir in noodles and turkey. Turn slow cooker to high setting; cover and cook for one additional hour.

Serves 6

TOMATO-TORTELLINI SOUP

AMY COOPER
LEBANON, MO

Mom enjoyed this soup at a restaurant. She began to experiment and came up with her own version...we think it's even better!

- **12-oz. pkg. frozen cheese tortellini, uncooked**
- **28-oz. can crushed tomatoes**
- **28-oz. can Italian-style diced tomatoes**
- **6-oz. can tomato paste**
- **2 c. half-and-half**
- **1 c. milk**
- **1 t. kosher salt**
- **1 T. pepper, or to taste**
- **Garnish: grated Parmesan cheese**

Fill a stockpot with water; bring to a rolling boil over medium-high heat. Add tortellini; return to a boil. Remove from heat and let stand until tortellini float, 15 to 20 minutes; drain. Meanwhile, in a separate stockpot, combine remaining ingredients except garnish; bring to a simmer. Add cooked tortellini; stir. Garnish with Parmesan cheese.

Serves 3 to 4

HEARTY POTATO SOUP

TERESA POTTER
BRANSON, MO

My very own version of a wonderful soup that my husband and I used to enjoy at a special hometown restaurant.

- **6 potatoes, peeled and diced**
- **1/4 c. onion, minced**
- **salt and pepper**
- **10-3/4 oz. can cream of celery soup**
- **1 qt. milk**
- **3 to 4 c. instant potato flakes**

Place potatoes, onion, salt and pepper in a large saucepan; add enough water to cover. Bring to a boil over medium heat. Cover and cook for about 15 minutes, until potatoes are tender. Mash very lightly with a potato masher; do not drain. Add soup and mix well; add milk. When hot, stir in instant potatoes gradually until desired thickness is achieved. Simmer about 10 minutes before serving.

Serves 4

GARLIC POTATO SOUP & GARLIC TOAST

TERESA ELLER
KANSAS CITY, MO

I love this soup on a snowy cold winter day. It really hits the spot! For an even heartier soup, add some diced, cooked ham or chicken.

6 potatoes, peeled and cubed
1/4 c. butter
1/2 c. celery, chopped
1/2 c. onion, chopped
1 t. garlic powder, or to taste
4 to 6 c. milk
1/2 to 3/4 c. pasteurized process cheese, cubed

In a soup pot, cover potatoes with water. Bring to a boil over medium-high heat; cook until potatoes are tender. Drain; add butter, celery, onion, garlic powder and milk to desired consistency. Simmer over medium heat, stirring occasionally, until celery and onion are tender; do not boil. Add cheese; stir until melted. Serve soup with Garlic Toast.

Garlic Toast:

GARLIC TOAST
1/4 c. butter
1 t. garlic powder
1 loaf French bread, sliced

Mix butter with garlic powder until creamy. Spread on sliced bread; place on an ungreased baking sheet. Bake at 350 degrees for 5 minutes, or until lightly toasted.

Serves 4 to 6

JASON'S FAVORITE PEA SOUP

STORMY SNOW
BRANSON, MO

My son has loved this hearty pea soup recipe since he was young. I like to serve it with ham sandwiches for a complete meal.

16-oz. pkg. dried split peas
2 14-1/2 oz. cans low-sodium chicken broth
1/2 c. water
1/2 c. celery, chopped
1/4 t. garlic powder
1/4 t. dried marjoram
1/4 t. dried thyme
1/8 t. pepper
1/2 to 3/4 lb. cooked ham, diced
1 potato, peeled and diced
2 to 3 carrots, peeled and diced salt to taste
Optional: 1/2 c. whipping cream

In a Dutch oven, cover peas with broth and water. Over medium-high heat, bring to a boil; boil for 2 minutes. Remove from heat; cover and let stand for one hour. Return to stovetop; add celery and seasonings. Return to a boil; cover, reduce heat to low and simmer for 2 hours, stirring occasionally. Add an additional cup of water if needed. Add ham, potato and carrots. Simmer for 45 minutes, stirring occasionally. Add salt to taste. For a creamier texture, stir in cream during the last 15 minutes of cooking time.

Serves 6 to 8

ITALIAN BEEF HOAGIES

MICHELLE RILEY
BARNHART, MO

We like to spread garlic butter on warm, toasted hoagie rolls before adding beef...scrumptious!

3 to 4-lb. beef chuck roast
2.6-oz. pkgs. zesty Italian salad dressing mix
2 c. water
24-oz. jar pepperoncinis, drained and liquid reserved
15 to 18 hoagie rolls, toasted and split
Garnish: shredded provolone cheese

Slice roast across the grain into 4 pieces and trim any fat. Place in bottom of a slow cooker. Mix together dressing mix and water; pour over beef. Cover and cook on low setting for 8 to 10 hours, until tender; use forks to shred beef in slow cooker. Slice pepperoncinis into rings and add to slow cooker along with reserved liquid from jar. Cover and cook for a few more minutes, until heated through. Serve beef on toasted rolls, topped with cheese.

Serves 15 to 18

POTATO-LEEK SOUP

ANGELA SCHUBBE
SAINT CHARLES, MO

My family loves this delicious, comforting soup for lunch with a crisp tossed salad.

8 potatoes, peeled and diced
2 c. chicken broth
1 white onion, diced
1 leek, white part only, diced
3 stalks celery, diced
2 T. butter
2 c. milk, warmed
2 t. sea salt, or to taste
2 t. pepper

In a large stockpot over high heat, combine potatoes and broth; cook until tender. Meanwhile, in a separate skillet over medium heat, sauté onion, leek and celery in butter until translucent. When potatoes are tender, stir in onion mixture, milk and seasonings. Using a potato masher, gently mash half of the potatoes in the stockpot to desired texture. Warm through over low heat.

Serves 9 to 10

SPINACH BISQUE

KENDRA CORDES
ARNOLD, MO

As a mother of three boys, I have found it is really hard to get some kids to eat their veggies. My kids love this bisque and actually beg me to make it! It's great served with sandwiches or by itself with crackers.

26-oz. can cream of mushroom soup
1 c. milk
2 10-oz. pkgs. frozen chopped spinach, thawed and drained
1 onion, diced
12-oz. pkg. Shredded mozzarella cheese
14-1/2 oz. can beef broth
salt and pepper to taste

In a large soup pot over medium heat, combine soup and milk; stir until smooth. Add spinach and onion. Once spinach is warmed through, add mozzarella cheese. Add beef broth to desired consistency; add salt and pepper to taste. Cook until cheese is just melted; serve immediately.

Serves 2 to 4

SO-EASY PORK FRITTERS

ELENA NELSON
CONCORDIA, MO

This is my husband's favorite meal. I created this recipe to mimic a menu item at our favorite restaurant. These fritters are excellent in a sandwich too.

1 lb. pork tenderloin, sliced
1/2-inch thick
1 egg, beaten
3 T. milk
1 sleeve saltine crackers, finely crushed
3/4 c. all-purpose flour
1 t. salt
1/2 t. pepper
oil for frying

Flatten pork with a meat mallet; set aside. Place egg and milk in a small bowl and blend well. Combine cracker crumbs, flour and seasonings in a separate bowl. Dip pork slices into egg mixture, then press in crumb mixture until well coated. Heat 1/2 inch of oil in a skillet over medium-high heat. Add pork slices; fry until deep golden on both sides and no longer pink in the middle, turning as needed.

Serves 4

PARTY-PERFECT PULLED PORK

PENNY SHERMAN
AVA, MO

This is my go-to slow-cooker recipe all fall and winter for football parties, holiday parties, you name it! It's so easy, yet feeds a crowd. Just add chips and coleslaw.

1-1/2 t. smoked paprika
1 t. cayenne pepper
1 t. dried thyme
1 t. garlic powder
1/2 t. salt
2 t. pepper
5-lb. boneless pork shoulder roast
1 c. water
16 to 20 sandwich buns, split
Garnish: favorite barbecue sauce

Combine all seasonings in a small bowl; rub evenly over all sides of roast. Add roast to a 6-quart slow cooker; add water. Cover and cook on low setting for 6 to 8 hours, or on high setting for 4 to 5 hours, until roast is very tender. Remove roast to a platter; let stand for 10 to 15 minutes. Shred with 2 forks. Serve pork in buns, topped with barbecue sauce.

Serves 16 to 20

SAUSAGE BEAN GUMBO

JO CLINE
SMITHVILLE, MO

Quick & easy...ready in thirty minutes!

1 lb. smoked pork sausage link, sliced
3 15-1/2 oz. cans Great Northern beans
15-1/2 oz. can diced tomatoes with sweet onions
1 stalk celery, diced
1/2 c. green pepper, diced
1/2 t. garlic powder
1/4 t. pepper
Optional: fresh cilantro, chopped

In a large saucepan over low heat, combine all ingredients except garnish; do not drain vegetables. Cover and simmer for about 30 minutes, stirring occasionally. Sprinkle servings with cilantro, if desired.

Serves 4

KITCHEN CABINET MILD WHITE CHILI

BECKY HALL
BELTON, MO

This recipe was created on a cold night with ingredients from the kitchen cabinet. It can easily be spiced up with a can of diced chiles or chopped jalapeño peppers.

2 15-1/2 oz. cans great Northern beans
Optional: 4-1/2 oz. can diced green chiles
14-oz. can chicken broth
1 T. dried, minced onion
1 T. red pepper flakes
1-1/2 t. dried, minced garlic
1 t. ground cumin
1/2 t. dried oregano
1/8 t. cayenne pepper
1/8 t. ground cloves
1-1/2 c. cooked chicken, chopped
4-oz. can sliced mushrooms, drained
1 c. shredded sharp Cheddar cheese

In a Dutch oven, combine all ingredients except chicken, mushrooms and cheese. Cook over medium heat for 5 minutes; bring to a boil. Reduce heat and simmer 5 minutes. Add chicken and mushrooms; simmer, uncovered, for 8 to 10 minutes, until heated through. Serve with cheese.

Serves 4

KITCHEN TIP

A new twist on casserole toppers... try crushed veggie, chicken or cheese-flavored crackers combined with fresh or dried herbs and melted butter. Sprinkle on top before baking for a delicious crunch.

SHREDDED BEEF SANDWICHES

SHARON BEACH
POTOSI, MO

I love to toast the split buns in the oven for a few minutes before serving.

Pour pepperoncini with liquid into a 5-quart slow cooker; add roast. Mix together spices, salt and pepper in a small bowl; sprinkle over roast. Add water and onion. Cover and cook on low setting for 8 to 9 hours, until meat is tender. Remove roast; shred using 2 forks. Return meat to slow cooker; mix well. Using a slotted spoon, place meat on buns.

Serves 10 to 12

12-oz. jar sliced pepperoncini
4-lb. beef chuck roast
1-3/4 t. dried basil
1-1/2 t. dried oregano
1-1/2 t. garlic powder
1-1/4 t. salt
1/4 t. pepper
1/4 c. water
1 onion, sliced
10 to 12 sandwich buns, split and toasted

HOAGIE HAMBURGER BOATS

KISHA LANDEROS
PACIFIC, MO

This is a dish my brother and I would always request! My mom made these sandwiches for us for busy afternoons and school nights. Simple to make, very filling and easy clean-up.

Slice off the tops of hoagie rolls. Pull out the centers of rolls to create "boats." Set aside tops and bread pieces. In a skillet over medium heat, brown beef; drain. Stir in soup and bread pieces; season with salt and pepper. Simmer for a few minutes, until heated through. Place rolls on a baking sheet; spoon beef mixture into rolls. Add cheese slices; replace tops onto rolls. Bake at 400 degrees for 10 to 15 minutes, until cheese is melted.

Serves 6

6 hoagie rolls
1 to 1-1/2 lbs. ground beef
10-3/4 oz. can cream of mushroom soup
salt and pepper to taste
6 slices American cheese

CHAPTER FOUR

Missouri

Mains

FILL THEM UP WITH A STICK-TO-THE-RIBS MEAL THAT IS FULL OF FLAVOR AND HEARTY ENOUGH TO SATISFY EVEN THE BIGGEST APPETITE.

CREAMY SLOPPY JOES

JENITA DAVISON
LA PLATA, MO

My mom, who didn't especially care for tomato-based Sloppy Joes, shared this recipe with me many years ago. It's a nice change of pace and great comfort food.

- **1-1/2 lbs. ground beef**
- **Optional: 1/4 c. onion, diced**
- **10-3/4 oz. can cream of mushroom soup**
- **2 T. Worcestershire sauce**
- **1/4 c. catsup**
- **1/3 c. light brown sugar, packed**

In a large skillet over medium heat, brown beef with onion, if using; drain. Stir in remaining ingredients. Reduce heat to medium-low. Simmer until flavors are blended, about 10 minutes. Spoon onto buns or over slices of toast.

Serves 4

PRESENTATION

Make it easy for guests to mingle and chat...set up food at several tables instead of one big party buffet. Place hot foods on one table, chilled foods on another, sweets on yet another.

FABULOUS FLANK STEAK

SHERI KOHL
WENTZVILLE, MO

This marinade takes an everyday flank steak and elevates it to restaurant quality...a winner every time! Great for a quick family dinner with baked potatoes and a tossed salad.

- **2 to 3-lb. beef flank steak**
- **1/2 c. soy sauce**
- **1/4 c. Worcestershire sauce**
- **3 T. Dijon mustard**
- **1 T. pepper**
- **4 cloves garlic, minced**

Place steak in a shallow glass or plastic dish; set aside. Whisk together remaining ingredients in a small bowl; pour over steak. Cover and refrigerate overnight. Remove steak from marinade and pat dry; discard marinade. Grill or broil steak to desired doneness, about 4 minutes per side for medium-rare. Let stand 10 minutes; slice thinly on the diagonal.

Serves 4 to 6

HELFER FAMILY SPECIAL

BARB WISMANN
BALLWIN, MO

This recipe always makes me think of my mom, who first came up with it. She would serve it to my brother and me when we were kids. We served it to our kids and now our kids are serving it to theirs! We have all tweaked this dish from time to time, but the original is still quick and tasty.

- **1 c. frozen peas**
- **5-1/2 oz. pkg. macaroni & cheese, uncooked**
- **1/2 lb. ground beef**
- **salt and pepper to taste**

Set out peas to thaw slightly. Prepare macaroni & cheese according to package directions. Meanwhile, cook beef in a frying pan over medium heat until browned. Drain; add salt and pepper and set aside. Add peas directly to prepared macaroni & cheese and stir well; add beef and stir.

Serves 4 to 6

FAST & FANCY BEEF STIR-FRY

SHERI KOHL
WENTZVILLE, MO

A great quick and tasty meal for those busy weeknights. You can vary the veggies to your family's taste. Not a drop left over, ever! Serve with cooked rice and egg rolls.

1 to 2 T. oil
1 lb. beef flank steak, cut into thin strips
1 zucchini, sliced
1 lb. sliced mushrooms
8-oz. can sliced water chestnuts, drained
11.8-oz. bottle teriyaki baste & glaze sauce
Garnish: sweet-and-sour sauce

Heat oil in a large skillet over medium-high heat. Add steak strips; cook and stir until browned on both sides and cooked through. Remove steak to a plate; set aside. Add zucchini and mushrooms. Cook and stir for 3 to 4 minutes, to desired tenderness. Return steak to skillet; add water chestnuts and heat through. Stir in teriyaki sauce; heat through over low heat. Serve with sweet-and-sour sauce as desired.

Serves 4 to 6

SLOW-COOKED HAM MEAL

JENITA DAVISON
LA PLATA, MO

Creamy comfort food. This smells wonderful while it's cooking!

8 to 12 slices cooked ham, divided
32-oz. pkg. frozen potato puffs, thawed and divided
8-oz. pkg. shredded Cheddar cheese, divided
10-3/4 oz. can cream of mushroom or celery soup, divided
1/2 c. onion, diced and divided
pepper to taste

Spray a 6-quart slow cooker with non-stick vegetable spray. Layer half of each ingredient in the order listed. Repeat layers. Cover and cook on low setting for 6 to 8 hours, or on high setting for 4 hours. (Low setting will not stick as easily.) Stir occasionally along the sides during last half of cooking time.

Makes 6 servings

Chicken & Rotini Stir-Fry, p 92

Whether you are looking for a quick-to-make breakfast dish to start the day off right, no-fuss party fare for those special guests, satisfying soups and sandwiches for the perfect lunch, main dishes to bring them to the table fast, or a sweet little something to savor at the end of the meal, you'll love these recipes from the amazing cooks in beautiful Missouri.

led Beef Sandwiches, p 75

Tex-Mex Egg Puffs, p 27

ent Breakfast Casserole, p 16

Fresh Strawberry Pie, p 145

Robert's Corn Dip, p 124

Garden-Style Fettuccine, p 111

Aunt Kornye's Cinnamon Rolls, p 28

165-Dollar Blackberry-Apple Pie, p 144

Honey-Mustard Short Ribs, p 94

Hamburger Crunch, p 109

n Parmesan Roasted Potatoes, p 46

Bonnie's Chicken Noodle Soup, p 62

ef Porcucpine Meatballs, p 112

Irish Corned Beef Dinner, p 112

Pasta a la Drini, p 109

BBQ Chicken Pizza, p 108

Pulled BBQ Chicken, p 54

Kitchen Cabinet Mild White Chili, p 74

Potato-Leek Soup, p 71

Pecan Flapjacks, p 13

Pork Chops with Apple Stuffing, p 108

So-Easy Pork Fritters, p 73

Mike's Irresistible Italian Chops, p 110

Nutty Brown Sugar Muffins, p 25

BUSY MOM'S BISCUIT CHEESEBURGER PIZZA

RACHEL ROWDEN
FESTUS, MO

This is a go-to for my family of four on those nights we have softball and tee ball practice. My 12-year-old daughter Isabella and 6-year-old daughter Carly both love this recipe.

1 lb ground beef
1 T. dried, minced onion
salt and pepper to taste
10-3/4 oz. can Cheddar cheese soup
16-oz. tube refrigerated biscuits
1 c. shredded Cheddar cheese
Garnish: cheeseburger condiments

Brown beef in a skillet with onion; drain and season with salt and pepper. Stir in soup; set aside. Stretch biscuits and press together to form a crust; place on a baking sheet sprayed with non-stick vegetable spray. Top crust with beef mixture; sprinkle evenly with cheese. Bake at 350 degrees for 10 minutes, or until crust is golden and cheese is melted. Cut into squares; serve with your favorite condiments.

Serves 8

CRUMBED HONEY MUSTARD PORK CHOPS

SARINA SKIDMORE
URBANA, MO

Just three ingredients...what could be easier?

8-oz. pkg. cornbread stuffing mix
1/2 c. honey mustard
4 to 6 pork chops

Pour stuffing mix into a shallow dish; set aside. Brush mustard over both sides of each pork chop; coat with stuffing mix. Arrange pork chops on a lightly greased baking sheet. Bake, uncovered, at 350 degrees for 20 minutes, or until juices run clear.

Serves 4 to 6.

SAUSAGE, KALE & POTATO CASSEROLE

MARY BETTUCHY
SAINT ROBERT, MO

This is my go-to recipe whenever I'm planning ahead for a busy week. The leftovers are just as good as when it first comes out of the oven, so I know we won't mind eating it again if I don't have time to cook! I like to use turkey kielbasa and 2% milk shredded cheese for a little less fat.

4 lbs. russet potatoes, peeled, and cut into chunks
1 T. salt
1/4 c. butter, sliced
3/4 c. milk
1 T. olive oil
1 onion, halved and thinly sliced
1 clove garlic, minced
1/2 c. cider vinegar
1/2 c. water
2 bunches fresh kale, coarsely chopped and stems trimmed
3/4 lb. Kielbasa or smoked pork sausage, sliced 1/2-inch thick
8-oz. pkg. shredded Monterey Jack or Cheddar cheese

In a large pot over high heat, cook potatoes in boiling water for 20 to 30 minutes, until tender; drain. Add salt and butter; mash until butter is well mixed. Add milk; continue to mash until creamy and smooth, adding more milk if needed. Set aside. Meanwhile, in a large stockpot, heat oil over medium-high heat until shimmering. Add onion and sauté for about 5 minutes, until translucent. Add garlic; cook one minute more. Add vinegar, water and kale; reduce heat to medium. Cover and cook for 10 to 15 minutes, stirring occasionally, until kale is wilted and soft. Spread mashed potatoes in the bottom of a greased 3-quart casserole dish; spread kale mixture over potatoes. Top with sausage slices. Bake, uncovered, at 350 degrees for 30 minutes, or until heated through and sausage is lightly golden. Sprinkle with cheese; bake 5 minutes more, or until cheese is melted.

Serves 6 to 8

DUTCH SPARERIBS & DUMPLINGS

SHARON CRIDER
LEBANON, MO

Dumplings are stick-to-your-ribs fall fare!

- 3 lbs. country-style pork spareribs
- 29-oz. can sauerkraut, drained and rinsed
- 2 tart apples, cored, peeled and cut into wedges
- 1 c. onion, chopped
- 2 t. seasoned salt
- 1/2 t. seasoned pepper
- 1/4 t. caraway seed

Slice spareribs into serving portions and trim any excess fat; place in a lightly greased slow cooker. Top ribs with sauerkraut, apples and onion; sprinkle with seasonings. Cover and cook on low setting for 8 hours, or until ribs are very tender when pierced. Remove excess liquid above sauerkraut with a bulb baster. Drop dumplings by heaping tablespoonfuls on top of sauerkraut. Cover and cook on high setting for 30 minutes, or until dumplings are fluffy.

Dumplings:

DUMPLINGS

- 2 c. all-purpose flour
- 2 t. baking powder
- 1 t. salt
- 1/2 t. caraway seed
- 1 egg
- 3/4 c. milk

Combine flour, baking powder and salt in a large bowl; stir in caraway seed. Beat egg in a cup with a fork; beat in milk. Pour all at once into flour mixture; stir until blended.

Serves 4 to 6

CHICKEN IN THE GARDEN

SUMMER PIEPER
KEARNEY, MO

A fix & forget meal featuring pantry staples. Choose instant brown rice to add whole-grain goodness, if you wish.

4 boneless, skinless chicken breasts, sliced into strips
1 T. oil
14-1/2 oz. can French-cut green beans, drained
4-oz. can sliced mushrooms, drained
1 t. garlic salt
salt and pepper to taste
14-1/2 oz. can chicken broth
1 t. dried basil
1-1/2 c. instant rice, uncooked
Optional: soy sauce to taste

In a skillet over medium heat, brown chicken in oil. Stir in green beans, mushrooms, garlic salt, salt and pepper. Add broth and basil; bring to a boil. Stir in uncooked rice. Turn to low heat; cover and cook for 15 minutes, or until broth is absorbed and rice is cooked. Sprinkle with soy sauce, if desired.

Serves 4 to 6

KITCHEN TIP

A pat of homemade garlic butter really adds flavor to warm bread or steamed vegetables. Blend equal parts of softened butter and olive oil, then stir in finely chopped garlic to taste...so easy!

BAKED TILAPIA & PEPPERS

MARYBETH HUNTON
JEFFERSON CITY, MO

My family has always enjoyed fried fish, so I was pleasantly surprised when they liked this baked fish dish. My husband isn't fond of any type of bell peppers...he likes the fish baked with them, he just doesn't eat the peppers!

1 lemon
salt and pepper to taste
1 green pepper, cut in strips
1 red pepper, cut in strips
1 yellow pepper, cut in strips
1/2 c. white wine or water
2 to 3 t. olive oil
4 tilapia fillets

Grate zest from lemon. Mix zest with salt and pepper in a small bowl; set aside. Cover a 15"x10" jelly-roll pan with aluminum foil. Grease lightly; place peppers on foil. Cut lemon in half; squeeze 1/4 cup juice from lemon. Drizzle peppers with wine or water, lemon juice and olive oil. Sprinkle with salt and pepper; toss gently. Arrange fish fillets on top; sprinkle fish with lemon zest mixture. Slice lemon halves very thinly; top each fillet with 2 to 3 lemon slices. Fold up foil and seal tightly. Bake at 350 degrees for 20 minutes, or until fish flakes easily with a fork.

Serves 4

CHICKEN & ROTINI STIR-FRY

MARY KELLY
JEFFERSON CITY, MO

This very tasty, light recipe is so easy to make. You're gonna love it!

- **2-1/2 c. rotini pasta, uncooked**
- **2 T. olive oil**
- **2 boneless, skinless chicken breasts, cut into strips**
- **1 c. broccoli flowerets**
- **1/2 c. red onion, sliced**
- **1 c. carrots, peeled and cut into curls with a vegetable peeler**
- **1/4 c. water**
- **1/2 t. chicken bouillon granules**
- **1/2 t. fresh tarragon, snipped**
- **2 T. grated Parmesan cheese**

Cook pasta as directed on package; drain. Meanwhile, heat oil in a large skillet over medium-high heat. Add chicken, broccoli, onion and carrots. Cook and stir until broccoli is crisp-tender, about 10 minutes. Add water, bouillon and tarragon; cook and stir until chicken is cooked through. Add pasta and cheese. Toss to coat; serve immediately.

Serves 4 to 6

CHICKEN-BROCCOLI ROTINI SALAD

DEBBIE CUTELLI
SAINT LOUIS, MO

I've served this delicious salad often at ladies' luncheons and showers.

2-1/2 c. rotini pasta, uncooked
2 c. cooked chicken, cubed
1/2 c. Italian salad dressing
2 c. broccoli, cut into bite-size flowerets
1/2 c. red pepper, chopped

Cook pasta according to package directions; drain and rinse with cold water. In a large bowl, mix pasta with chicken and Italian salad dressing. Cover and refrigerate for one hour. Add broccoli, red pepper and Parmesan Dressing; toss to mix. Cover and refrigerate until serving time.

Parmesan Dressing

1 c. grated Parmesan cheese
1/2 c. olive oil
2 T. lemon juice
1/8 t. dried basil

Parmesan Dressing

In a bowl, whisk all ingredients together.

Serves 6

LAZY-DAY GRILLED RIBS

PENNY SHERMAN
AVA, MO

Pop these spicy ribs in the oven for the afternoon, then grill briefly before dinnertime...what could be simpler for a weekend meal?

- **2-1/2 T. coarse salt**
- **1-1/2 T. light brown sugar, packed**
- **1-1/2 T. chili powder**
- **3/4 t. coarse pepper**
- **4 to 4-1/2 lbs. pork spareribs, cut into serving-size pieces**
- **1 c. tangy barbecue sauce, divided**

In a small bowl, mix together salt, brown sugar and spices. Rub salt mixture evenly over both sides of ribs. Transfer ribs, bone-side down, and slightly overlapping, to a rimmed baking sheet. Cover tightly with aluminum foil. Bake at 300 degrees for 2-1/2 to 3 hours, until tender. Unwrap ribs and place on an oiled grate over medium-high heat. Cook for 2 to 5 minutes per side, brushing with 1/2 cup barbecue sauce, until slightly blackened. Serve remaining sauce alongside ribs.

Serves 4 to 6

HONEY-MUSTARD SHORT RIBS

SARA TAYLOR
ROSEBUD, MO

All the fun of a Saturday night barbecue...with none of the effort.

- **3 to 4 lbs. bone-in beef short ribs**
- **salt and pepper to taste**
- **1 c. hickory smoke-flavored barbecue sauce**
- **3 T. honey**
- **1 T. Dijon mustard**
- **3 cloves garlic, minced**
- **2 T. cornstarch**
- **2 T. cold water**

Sprinkle ribs with salt and pepper; place in a slow cooker and set aside. Combine barbecue sauce, honey, mustard, garlic and additional salt and pepper, if desired; pour over ribs. Cover and cook on low setting for 6 to 7 hours. During the last 30 minutes of cooking, whisk cornstarch into water. Add to slow cooker, stirring until thickened.

Serves 4

KIDDIES' CHICKEN PACKETS

DAWN SMITH
CAPE GIRARDEAU, MO

I teach a children's cooking class, and for the finale the students prepare this recipe for their parents. These packets turn out perfectly every time, and the chicken is so tender and yummy! The parents are always so impressed. Serve right from the packet, if you like.

1 c. Italian salad dressing, divided
4 boneless, skinless chicken breasts
salt and pepper to taste
3 potatoes, thinly sliced
10 baby carrots, sliced
1 stalk celery, chopped
1 onion, sliced

Drizzle four 18-inch lengths of heavy-duty aluminum foil with one tablespoon salad dressing each. Season chicken breasts with salt and pepper. Layer each piece of foil with one chicken breast, one tablespoon salad dressing, potatoes divided between packets, one tablespoon salad dressing and remaining vegetables divided between packets. Drizzle with remaining salad dressing. Fold foil together to make packets; seal tightly but allow a little room at the top. Grill over medium-low heat for 45 minutes, until chicken juices run clear when pierced. Packets may also be baked on baking sheets at 350 degrees for 45 minutes.

Serves 4

GREEK CHICKEN SKILLET

KATIE WOLLGAST
FLORISSANT, MO

This recipe is really good, so colorful and fast for busy nights, and it uses some of my favorite vegetables. I like to garnish it with the works! I love it with polenta in the colder months because it is so warm and satisfying. It's good over pasta, couscous or rice too.

1 T. oil
1 lb. boneless, skinless chicken breast, sliced into thin strips
1 yellow pepper, cut into 3/4-inch pieces
1 green pepper, cut into 3/4-inch pieces
1 onion, cut into wedges
1/2 c. green onions, chopped and divided
1/4 lb. sliced mushrooms
2 cloves garlic, minced
14-1/2 oz. can diced tomatoes
8-oz. can tomato sauce
1 T. brown sugar, packed
1 T. dried basil
1/2 t. dried oregano
1/2 t. dried thyme
1 t. salt
cooked polenta, sliced
Garnish: crumbled feta cheese or shredded Parmesan cheese, sliced black olives
8-oz. container plain Greek yogurt
1 T. pesto sauce

Heat oil in a large skillet over medium heat. Add chicken; cook until golden on all sides. Add peppers, onion, 1/4 cup green onions, mushrooms and garlic; sauté until fragrant. Stir in tomatoes with juice, tomato sauce, brown sugar and seasonings. Bring to a boil; reduce heat to medium-low. Cover and simmer for 15 minutes, or until vegetables are tender. Serve over polenta; garnish with remaining onions and other toppings as desired. Combine yogurt and pesto sauce; serve on the side.

Serves 4

NUT-CRUSTED BAKED CHICKEN

MICAH TANNEHILL
SPRINGFIELD, MO

Everyone loves this supper...it's really good for any occasion! Just add rice pilaf and steamed, buttered broccoli for an elegant meal that's oh-so easy to prepare.

- **6-oz. pkg. cornbread stuffing mix**
- **1/4 c. almonds**
- **1/4 c. walnuts**
- **1/4 c. French fried onions**
- **1/2 t. pepper**
- **1 egg, beaten**
- **3 T. warm water**
- **10-3/4 oz. can cream of mushroom soup**
- **4 boneless, skinless chicken breasts**

Combine stuffing mix, almonds, walnuts, onions and pepper in a blender. Pulse mixture to the texture of cornmeal; place in a shallow bowl. In a separate shallow bowl, whisk egg and water together. Add soup to egg mixture and beat until well blended. Dip chicken breasts into egg mixture and then into stuffing mixture until well coated. Place in a greased 13"x9" baking pan. Bake, uncovered, at 400 degrees until chicken juices run clear when pierced, about 45 minutes.

Serves 4

DINNERTIME CONVERSATION

Missouri's culture blends elements from the Midwestern and Southern United States. The musical styles of ragtime, Kansas City jazz and Saint Louis blues developed in Missouri. The well-known Kansas City-style barbecue and lesser-known Saint Louis-style barbecue can be found across the state and beyond.

ITALIAN-STYLE POT ROAST

ROSEMARY KERNS
SAINT JOSEPH, MO

My kids love this roast, and the slow cooker makes it so simple.

1 onion, sliced
3 cloves garlic, minced
28-oz. can crushed tomatoes
2 T. balsamic vinegar
1 T. Worcestershire sauce
1 T. Italian seasoning
2 t. brown sugar, packed
salt and pepper to taste
2 to 3-lb. beef chuck roast

Blend together all ingredients except roast in a bowl. Pour half the mixture into a slow cooker and add roast; pour remaining mixture over top. Cover and cook on low setting for 6 to 8 hours.

Serves 6

BIEROCK CASSEROLE

RHONDA DARBRO
SHELL KNOB, MO

This is a quick & easy alternative to making individual bierock meat pies. The recipe can easily be divided between two 8"x8" pans...one to serve now and one to freeze for later, or to share with a neighbor!

2 lbs. lean ground beef
1 onion, chopped
1/2 head cabbage, shredded
salt and pepper to taste
2 8-oz. tubes refrigerated crescent rolls
2 c. shredded Cheddar cheese

In a skillet over medium heat, brown beef and onion; do not drain. Add cabbage; reduce heat to low and simmer for 20 minutes. Season to taste with salt and pepper. Spray a 13"x9" baking pan with non-stick vegetable spray. Press one tube of crescent rolls into the bottom of pan, sealing perforations. Spread beef mixture over rolls; sprinkle cheese over beef mixture. Top with remaining tube of crescent rolls, sealing perforations. Bake, uncovered, at 350 degrees for 30 minutes. Cut into squares to serve.

Serves 6 to 8

MOMMA RITA'S QUICK CASSEROLE

RITA BOMBERRY
DESOTO, MO

Being a busy mom of six kids, I invented this one-pot meal. Of course the kids love it, since it has lots of cheese in it!

Brown turkey with onion in a large stockpot over medium heat; drain. Add garlic powder and pepper to taste. Stir in green beans, corn and potatoes; add seasoned salt to taste. Heat through, stirring occasionally. Top with cheese slices as desired. Simmer over low heat about 10 minutes, until cheese is melted. Stir to combine.

Serves 6

1 lb. ground turkey
1/4 onion, diced garlic powder and pepper to taste
2 14-1/2 oz. cans green beans, drained
2 15-1/4 oz. cans corn, drained
2 15-oz. cans diced potatoes, drained
seasoned salt to taste
5 to 10 slices American cheese

SLOW-COOKER HONEY RIBS

DARCY ERICKSEN
INDEPENDENCE, MO

Hearty and full of flavor.

Combine all ingredients except ribs in a slow cooker; mix well. Add ribs and stir to coat. Cover and cook on low setting for 6 to 8 hours, or on high setting for 3 to 4 hours.

Serves 4

10-1/2 oz. can beef broth
3/4 c. water
3 T. soy sauce
2 T. maple syrup
2 T. honey
2 T. barbecue sauce
1/2 t. dry mustard
2 lbs. baby back pork ribs, cut into serving-size pieces

SALLY'S FRIED CABBAGE WITH SAUSAGE

SALLY DAVISON
FAYETTE, MO

This is a quick meal that I make almost weekly. When I've traveled to family homes and made this, everyone loves it and wants this easy recipe. It is a no-fail dish.

1/3 to 1/2 c. coconut oil or butter

1 head cabbage, shredded, or 12-oz. pkg. shredded coleslaw mix

1/2 to 3/4 c. onion, chopped

14-1/2 oz. can diced tomatoes, plain or with green chiles

1 lb. smoked pork or turkey sausage, sliced into rounds

1/2 t. salt

1/2 t. pepper

Melt coconut oil or butter in a large skillet over medium heat. Add cabbage and onion; cook for about 5 minutes, stirring often to prevent sticking. Add tomatoes with juice, sausage and seasonings. Cover and simmer over medium-low heat for 15 to 20 minutes, stirring occasionally.

Serves 2 to 4

HEAVENLY BEEF BRISKET

KIM AHMU
INDEPENDENCE, MO

An easy dinner for Sunday after church...it's a family favorite! We enjoy this scrumptious brisket with either potatoes or rice, topped with gravy made from the delicious juices in the slow cooker.

1 lb. carrots, peeled
Optional: 1 onion, sliced and divided
5 to 6-lb. beef brisket, trimmed
salt, pepper, onion powder and garlic powder to taste
1 c. water

Place carrots in a single layer on a large piece of heavy-duty aluminum foil. Top with half of onion slices, if desired. Sprinkle brisket on both sides with salt, pepper, onion powder and garlic powder. Place brisket on top of carrots. If necessary, cut brisket in half to fit in your slow cooker; layer the halves on top of each other. Place remaining onion slices on top, if using. Lay another piece of foil on top; fold edges to seal tight. Pour water into a large slow cooker; add foil packet. Cover and cook for 8 hours on low setting, or 4 to 5 hours on high setting.

Serves 4 to 6

HEALTHY SKILLET TACOS

ROBBI COURTAWAY
WEBSTER GROVES, MO

There are lots of recipes for skillet tacos out there, but none really fit our family's taste. So I adapted my own. Add cheese or not...the flavor is excellent without it!

1 T. oil
1/2 lb. lean ground beef
1 onion, chopped
14-1/2 oz. can petite diced tomatoes
1/2 c. chicken broth
1-1/4 oz. pkg. taco seasoning mix
1-1/2 c. frozen corn or canned sweet corn & diced peppers
15-1/2 oz. can small red beans drained and rinsed, or 15-oz. can hot or mild chili beans
Optional: 1/2 c. shredded Cheddar or Monterey Jack cheese
Garnish: crushed tortilla chips

Heat oil in a large skillet over medium heat; add beef and onion. Cook until beef is browned and onion is golden; drain. Stir in tomatoes with juice, chicken broth and taco seasoning; stir in corn and beans. Simmer over low heat until hot and bubbly, stirring occasionally. Stir in cheese, if desired. Top with crushed tortilla chips.

Serves 4 to 6

SMOTHERED MUSHROOM PORK CHOPS

KATHLEEN FETH
UNION, MO

These pork chops are fork-tender! I created this recipe myself and my family loves it. I include a copy of it in all bridal shower cards. If you use 2 cans of mushroom soup, the chops make their own gravy.

4 to 6 pork chops
celery salt, salt and pepper to taste
1 to 2 10-3/4 oz. cans cream of mushroom or golden mushroom soup
4-oz. can mushroom pieces, drained

Arrange pork chops in a greased 13"x9" baking pan; sprinkle with seasonings. Spread soup over chops; top with mushrooms. Cover pan tightly with aluminum foil. Bake at 350 degrees for about 45 minutes. To check for doneness, lift one corner back; steam will be hot. Let stand about 5 minutes before serving.

Serves 4 to 6

PRESTON'S ZUCCHINI STIR-FRY

LISA ELLSWORTH
SPARTA, MO

My husband Preston came up with this delicious dish one day while trying to figure out new ways of dealing with an abundance of zucchini. It's fast, inexpensive and very tasty...even the kids love it!

1 lb. ground beef
1 to 2 zucchini, cut into bite-size pieces
1 onion, chopped
1-1/2 c. water
1-1/2 c. instant rice, uncooked
Worcestershire sauce or soy sauce to taste

Add beef, zucchini and onion to a skillet. Cook over medium-high heat until beef is browned and vegetables are tender; drain. Add water and rice; bring to a boil. Remove from heat. Cover and let stand until water is absorbed and rice is tender, about 5 minutes. Add desired sauce to taste.

Serves 4

GRANDMA'S BEEF CASSEROLE

EVA JO HOYLE
MEXICO, MO

My grandmother would put this recipe in the slow cooker on fall Saturdays when we were raking leaves or picking apples at the orchard. It always smelled so good when we came inside!

- **2 lbs. stew beef cubes**
- **1/4 c. all-purpose flour**
- **10-3/4 oz. can cream of mushroom soup**
- **1.35-oz. pkg. onion soup mix**
- **4-oz. can whole mushrooms, drained**
- **1/2 c. red wine or beef broth**
- **12-oz. pkg. medium egg noodles, cooked**

Put beef cubes in a plastic zipping bag. Add flour; seal bag and shake to coat well. Brown beef in a heavy skillet that has been sprayed with non-stick vegetable spray; drain. In a slow cooker, combine beef with remaining ingredients except noodles. Cover and cook on low setting for 8 to 10 hours, or on high setting for 5 to 6 hours. To serve, spoon over cooked noodles.

Serves 6

PINEAPPLE CHICKEN

BETHANY HENDRIX
SPRINGFIELD, MO

My favorite lazy-day meal...a perfect reminder of warmer summer weather when the leaves start falling and the air gets crisp.

- **1 onion, chopped**
- **3 to 4 boneless, skinless chicken breasts**
- **20-oz. can pineapple rings**
- **2 T. soy sauce**
- **1/2 c. chicken broth**
- **cooked rice**

Place onion in a slow cooker; top onion with chicken. Add pineapple with juice to slow cooker; add soy sauce and broth. Cover and cook on low setting for 6 to 8 hours, until chicken is no longer pink in the center. Serve chicken, pineapple and juices over rice.

Serves 4 to 5

APPLE CIDER PORK CHOPS

VICKI WALSH
KANSAS CITY, MO

This recipe has become a favorite of ours, especially in the fall. It makes the whole house smell of apples and cinnamon.

- **4 to 6 thin pork chops**
- **1 c. chicken broth**
- **2 c. apple cider or apple juice**
- **1/4 t. celery seed**
- **1/4 c. brown sugar, packed**
- **1 t. cinnamon**
- **1 apple, cored and sliced**

Arrange pork chops in a single layer in a slow cooker. Pour broth over chops. Add apple cider or juice; sprinkle with celery seed. Cover and cook on low setting for 5 to 6 hours, until chops are tender. Add brown sugar, cinnamon and apple. Cover and cook on high setting for 30 to 45 minutes longer.

Serves 4

LATIN FUSION SPAGHETTI

SAMANTHA BOLEN
BRANSON, MO

We enjoy Spanish and Italian foods, so my hubby and I decided to fuse the two together! This dish is so good, and friends & family love it too.

- **16-oz. pkg. spaghetti, uncooked**
- **1 T. oil**
- **1 lb. Spanish-style chorizo pork sausage, thinly sliced**
- **32-oz. jar garden vegetable pasta sauce**
- **1-1/2 c. black bean and corn salsa**
- **2 c. shredded sharp Cheddar cheese**

Cook spaghetti according to package directions; drain. Meanwhile, add oil to a deep skillet; cook sausage in oil over medium-high heat, about 5 minutes per side, until browned. Drain. Lower heat to medium; add pasta sauce and salsa. Mix well; simmer for 10 to 12 minutes. Add drained spaghetti to sauce; cook over low heat for an additional 15 minutes. Garnish individual servings with cheese.

Serves 4

SPINACH & CHEESE NOODLES

KAREN FARR
WARSAW, MO

So easy to prepare in the slow cooker, and good enough for company!

- **2 T. butter**
- **1/3 c. all-purpose flour**
- **2-1/2 c. milk**
- **15-oz. container ricotta cheese**
- **10-oz. pkg. frozen spinach, thawed and drained**
- **3 T. Dijon mustard**
- **1 t. salt**
- **pepper to taste**
- **16-oz. pkg. wide egg noodles, uncooked**
- **1/4 c. grated Parmesan cheese**

Melt butter in a large saucepan over medium heat. Whisk in flour; add milk, ricotta cheese, spinach, mustard, salt and pepper. Set aside. Spray the inside of a 4-quart slow cooker with non-stick vegetable spray; add uncooked noodles. Pour in spinach mixture. Top with Parmesan cheese. Cover and cook on high setting for 2 to 4 hours, or until noodles are tender.

Serves 6

MOMMA JEWELL'S APPLESAUCE MEATLOAF

PATRICIA PARKER
CABOOL, MO

My mother was the head cook at a nursing home for many years. She would multiply recipes up to feed a hundred people. This is one of the favorites she made for the residents at the nursing home, and for her family too.

2 lbs. ground beef
1 egg, beaten
3/4 c. applesauce
1 c. dry bread crumbs
1 c. whole milk
1 t. salt
pepper to taste
1/2 c. catsup
3 T. brown sugar, packed
1 T. mustard

In a large bowl, combine beef, egg, applesauce, bread crumbs, milk, salt and pepper. Mix well; shape into a loaf. Place in an ungreased 13"x9" baking pan. In a separate bowl, combine remaining ingredients; spread over meatloaf. Bake, uncovered, at 350 degrees for one hour.

Serves 8 to 10

DINNERTIME CONVERSATION

Harry Truman was the only U.S. President to hail from Missouri. After he left the White House in 1953, he and his wife Bess moved back to the Independence home they shared with his mother-in-law and lived off his $112.56 monthly Army pension.

BBQ CHICKEN PIZZA

GINNY BONE
SAINT PETERS, MO

With only 5 ingredients, this is a scrumptious hurry-up meal your family will absolutely love.

- **12-inch Italian pizza crust**
- **3 c. cooked chicken, shredded**
- **1 c. barbecue sauce**
- **1 c. shredded mozzarella cheese**
- **1/2 c. shredded Cheddar cheese**

Place pizza crust on a lightly greased 12" round pizza pan. Combine chicken and barbecue sauce; spread on pizza crust. Sprinkle with cheeses. Bake at 450 degrees for 8 to 10 minutes, or until cheeses melt and crust is crisp.

Serves 4

PORK CHOPS WITH APPLE STUFFING

SHERRY LAMB NOBLE
KENNETT, MO

This tastes so good with a side of steamed green beans.

- **1 T. olive oil**
- **3 T. butter, divided**
- **5 boneless pork chops**
- **1 apple, cored and chopped**
- **1/2 c. onion, chopped**
- **1-2/3 c. water**
- **6-oz. pkg. stuffing mix**

Heat oil and one tablespoon butter in a large skillet over medium heat. Add pork chops; cook for 8 to 10 minutes, turning once, until cooked through. Remove chops; cover to keep warm. Melt remaining butter in skillet; add apple and onion. Cook for 3 to 5 minutes, stirring occasionally, until tender. Add water; bring to a boil. Stir in stuffing mix; remove from heat. Arrange chops over stuffing mixture; cover and let stand for 5 minutes before serving.

Serves 5

PASTA A LA DRINI

CATHERINE ALESANDRINI
FRENCH VILLAGE, MO

This is a great, healthy one-pot meal that's on the table in 30 minutes. It's so versatile...add any herbs or seasonings your family likes.

- **16-oz. pkg. Italian turkey sausage links**
- **28-oz. can fire-roasted diced tomatoes**
- **1/8 t. red pepper flakes**
- **dried oregano and dried basil to taste**
- **10-oz. pkg. frozen broccoli, cooked**
- **16-oz. pkg. whole-wheat penne pasta, cooked**

Place sausages on a grill pan over medium heat. Cook until browned and no longer pink in the center; remove from pan and let cool. In a large skillet over medium heat, combine tomatoes with juice and seasonings; bring to a simmer. Slice sausages into bite-size pieces and add to sauce. Add broccoli and pasta to skillet. Return to a simmer and cook for 3 to 5 minutes, until heated through.

Serves 4 to 6

HAMBURGER CRUNCH

GAYLE ORTMEYER
JEFFERSON CITY, MO

If you have any leftovers, roll them up in flour tortillas for tasty burritos.

- **2 lbs. ground beef**
- **1 T. onion, minced**
- **2 10-3/4 oz. cans tomato soup**
- **1 t. chili powder**
- **4 c. corn chips**
- **8-oz. pkg. shredded Cheddar cheese**

Brown ground beef and onion together in a large skillet over medium heat; drain. Stir in soup and chili powder. Spread in an ungreased 13"x9" baking pan; top with corn chips. Bake, uncovered, at 350 degrees for 20 to 25 minutes. Remove from oven; sprinkle with cheese. Bake for an additional 5 minutes, until cheese melts.

Serves 6 to 8

MIKE'S IRRESISTIBLE ITALIAN CHOPS

LESLIE MCKINLEY
MACOMB, MO

My dad is a master at cooking meats, and this is one of his signature dishes! We enjoy these chops with buttered noodles, rice or couscous.

5 pork chops
1-1/2 onions, coarsely chopped
15-oz. can stewed tomatoes
1/3 c. oil
1-1/2 t. Italian seasoning
1-1/2 t. garlic powder
2 t. smoke-flavored cooking sauce
1/4 c. water

Layer chops and onions in a slow cooker; add tomatoes with juice and remaining ingredients. Cover and cook on low setting for 3 to 4 hours, until chops are tender.

Serves 5

EASY GARLIC CHICKEN

THERESA WEHMEYER
ROSEBUD, MO

My family loves this chicken, and so do I! The short list of ingredients is easy to remember when I'm at the grocery store wondering what to make for dinner.

4 boneless, skinless chicken breasts
1/3 c. mayonnaise
1/4 c. grated Parmesan cheese
3 to 4 T. savory herb & garlic soup mix
2 T. dry bread crumbs

Place chicken in a greased 11"x7" baking pan. In a small bowl, combine mayonnaise, Parmesan cheese and soup mix. Spread chicken with mayonnaise mixture; sprinkle with bread crumbs. Bake, uncovered, at 400 degrees for 20 to 25 minutes, until chicken juices run clear when pierced.

Serves 4

GARDEN-STYLE FETTUCCINI

LISA HAYS
CROCKER, MO

What a delicious, nutritious meatless meal! It's packed full of veggies and yummy cheese...what more could you ask for?

- **1 zucchini, sliced 1/4-inch thick**
- **1 yellow squash, sliced 1/4-inch thick**
- **2 carrots, peeled and thinly sliced**
- **1-1/2 c. sliced mushrooms**
- **10-oz. pkg. frozen broccoli cuts**
- **4 green onions, sliced**
- **1 clove garlic, minced**
- **1/2 t. dried basil**
- **1/4 t. salt**
- **1/2 t. pepper**
- **1 c. grated Parmesan cheese**
- **12-oz. pkg. fettuccine pasta, cooked**
- **1 c. shredded mozzarella cheese**
- **1 c. milk**
- **2 egg yolks, beaten**

Place vegetables, seasonings and Parmesan cheese in a slow cooker. Cover and cook on high setting for 2 hours. Add remaining ingredients to slow cooker; stir well. Reduce heat to low setting; cover and cook an additional 15 to 30 minutes.

Serves 6 to 8

IRISH CORNED BEEF DINNER

APRIL JACOBS
CANTON, MO

Serve with rye bread and spicy mustard for a tasty meal!

3-lb. corned beef brisket
4 to 6 potatoes, quartered
1 lb. carrots, peeled, halved and cut into sticks
1 head cabbage, cut into wedges
2 onions, quartered
12-oz. can beer or non-alcoholic beer
1 bay leaf
2 to 3 c. water

Place brisket in a slow cooker. Arrange vegetables around brisket; add beer, bay leaf and enough water to cover. Cover and cook on low setting for 7 to 8 hours. Discard bay leaf. To serve, arrange vegetables on a large serving platter. Slice brisket and arrange over vegetables.

Serves 6

BEEF PORCUPINE MEATBALLS

TERRI LOCK
CARROLLTON, MO

As a teacher I need fast homestyle meals to seve to my family five before I leave for evening school events...this recipe is perfect.

8-oz. pkg. beef-flavored rice vermicelli mix
1 lb. ground beef
1 egg, beaten
2-1/2 c. water
cooked egg noodles

In a bowl, combine rice vermicelli mix, beef and egg, reserving seasoning packet from mix. Form mixture into one-inch balls. In a skillet over medium heat, cook meatballs, turning occasionally, until browned on all sides; drain. In a bowl, combine seasoning packet and water; pour over meatballs. Cover and simmer for 30 minutes, or until thickened and meatballs are no longer pink in the center. Serve meatballs and sauce over noodles.

Serves 6 to 8

SPUDS & SAUSAGES ONE-DISH

SHERI MOS
INDEPENDENCE, MO

I am notorious for throwing things together for dinner, usually to my family's dismay. This dish, though, was one everybody really liked! It's super easy, and now I get requests for it all the time. Very cozy and comforting.

4 c. boiling water
1 c. milk
1/4 c. butter, sliced
2 5-oz. pkgs. au gratin potatoes mix
16-oz. pkg. mini smoked sausages
Optional: shredded Cheddar cheese

Place boiling water, milk, butter and sauce mix in a greased 13"x9" baking pan; mix well. Stir in potatoes and sausages; top with cheese, if desired. Bake, uncovered, at 400 degrees for 35 minutes. Let stand for 5 minutes before serving.

Serves 4 to 6

CHAPTER FIVE

Pony Express

Appetizers & Snacks

WHETHER YOU ARE HAVING COMPANY OR JUST NEED A LITTLE SNACK TO HOLD YOU OVER UNTIL THE NEXT MEAL, YOU'LL FIND THESE RECIPES ARE GREAT FOR TAKING ON-THE-GO OR AS A FAVORITE APPETIZER.

TACO BISCUIT CUPS

LISA HARKE
OLD MONROE, MO

My teenage son and his friends eat these so fast I can't keep them around for long! I was looking for something to take to our church's potluck dinner, and this is what I came up with after looking at several recipes. I also add cream cheese on occasion. The biscuit cups also work great for spinach-artichoke feta cups as well.

- **1-1/2 lbs. ground beef**
- **1-1/4 oz. pkg taco seasoning mix**
- **3 8-oz. tubes refrigerated biscuits**
- **16-oz. jar salsa**
- **3 green onions, chopped**
- **4-oz. can chopped or sliced black olives, drained**
- **8-oz. pkg. shredded 3-cheese blend**

Brown beef in a skillet over medium heat; drain. Stir in seasoning mix; prepare according to packet instructions and remove from heat. Spray 48 mini muffin cups with non-stick vegetable spray. For each muffin cup, cut a biscuit in half; spread out each half with your fingers and press into a muffin cup. Continue until all biscuits are used. Fill each cup with a teaspoonful of beef mixture, 1/4 to 1/2 teaspoon salsa, onions, olives and a pinch of cheese. Bake at 350 degrees for 10 to 12 minutes, until biscuits are lightly golden. Cool slightly in muffin pans; remove to a tray for serving.

Makes 4 dozen

MARINATED MUSHROOMS

NORMA SEVIGNY
FENTON, MO

I've been making these zingy mushrooms for several years and everyone likes them. I keep these in a Mason jar in the refrigerator.

- **3/4 c. oil**
- **1/2 c. red wine vinegar**
- **1-1/2 t. salt**
- **1 t. sugar**
- **1/2 t. dried basil**
- **1/4 t. dried thyme**
- **6 peppercorns**
- **1 clove garlic, split**
- **1 bay leaf**
- **1-1/2 lbs. small mushrooms, trimmed**

In a large saucepan over medium heat, combine all ingredients except mushrooms. Heat to boiling; cover and simmer for 10 minutes. Add mushrooms; simmer for 3 minutes. Transfer mushrooms and liquid into a bowl. Cover and chill several hours to overnight, stirring occasionally. Drain; discard bay leaf. Serve as an appetizer or on a relish tray.

Makes 3-1/2 cups

BARBECUE HOT DOGS FOR A CROWD

MARIE KING
INDEPENDENCE, MO

A neighbor lady always used to bring these yummy hot dogs to church. She never had an exact recipe, just a barbecue sauce she and her husband enjoyed. I experimented with a few sauces and came up with this sauce that my kids love. This is such a great recipe for church potlucks or get-togethers, and is super easy to put together.

2 24-count pkgs. extra long hot dogs
13-1/2 oz. bottle catsup
18-oz. bottle barbecue sauce
18-oz. bottle hickory & brown sugar barbecue sauce
10-oz. bottle sweet-and-sour sauce

Place hot dogs in an ungreased 3-quart casserole dish. Bake, uncovered, at 425 degrees for 6 to 8 minutes. Cut each hot dog into quarters; return to dish. Reduce oven to 350 degrees. Generously drizzle hot dogs with catsup and barbecue sauces; drizzle less generously with sweet-and-sour sauce. Use a spatula to coat hot dogs with sauce. Bake, uncovered, at 350 degrees for 35 to 45 minutes, until sauce mixture is a thick glaze and hot dogs are plump, almost to bursting. Let cool and serve.

Serves 24

DINNERTIME CONVERSATION

The state of Missouri was named after a tribe of Sioux Indians of the state called the Missouris. The word "Missouri" means "wooden canoe people" or "he of the big canoe."

SPICY BEEF SPREAD

JESSICA CLARK
OAK GROVE, MO

My mother has made this recipe at the holidays for as long as I can remember. My sister and I have always scrambled to be the first one to dig in and to be the one to take leftovers home...if there were any, that is! Don't leave out the green onions, they're the best part!

8-oz. pkg. cream cheese, softened
1/4 c. mayonnaise
1 T. horseradish sauce
1-1/2 t. mustard
1/4 t. garlic salt
3-oz. pkg. thin-sliced corned beef, diced
4 green onions, green part only, diced
assorted crackers

In a large bowl, with an electric mixer on medium speed, beat cream cheese and mayonnaise until smooth. Beat in horseradish, mustard and garlic salt. Add corned beef and onions; mix thoroughly. Cover and refrigerate for at least one hour. Serve with crackers.

Serves 8

CRUNCHY CHICKEN ROLLS

AMY COATS
SAVANNAH, MO

This recipe is always a hit with family & friends. I got this recipe in high school cooking class and have been using it ever since! For variety, I sometimes like to replace the plain cream cheese with the garlic & herb kind.

12-oz. can chicken, drained and flaked
2 8-oz. pkgs. cream cheese, softened
3 T. fresh chives, chopped
2 8-oz. tubes refrigerated crescent rolls
2 T. butter, melted
4 c. chicken stuffing mix

In a large bowl, combine chicken, cream cheese and chives; blend well and set aside. Separate and flatten crescent rolls; top each triangle with one tablespoon of chicken mixture. Roll up triangles, sealing well. Dip each triangle into melted butter, then into stuffing mix. Place rolls on a sprayed baking sheet, stuffing-side up. Bake at 350 degrees for 10 to 15 minutes, until lightly golden.

Makes 16 rolls

JAN'S SIMPLE CHEESE BALL

JAN ABNEY
SALEM, MO

Every time our family gets together, they ask me to make my cheese ball. It's delicious...a real crowd-pleaser!

- 8-oz. pkg. cream cheese, room temperature
- 8-oz. pkg. shredded mild or sharp Cheddar cheese
- 1 t. garlic powder, or to taste
- 1 stalk celery, finely chopped
- 1/4 green pepper, finely chopped
- 1/4 onion, finely chopped
- 1 T. dried parsley
- 1 T. diced pimentos, drained
- Optional: 1/2 c. carrot, peeled and very finely chopped, or 1/2 c. walnuts, very finely chopped
- assorted snack crackers

In a large bowl, mix all ingredients except carrot or walnuts and crackers. Shape into one to 2 balls. Roll in chopped carrot or walnuts, or leave plain. Wrap in plastic wrap and chill. At serving time, place on a serving plate; surround with crackers.

Serves 8 to 10

JUST FOR FUN

Missouri has more than 6,000 known caves...including the one in Hannibal, where Tom Sawyer and Becky Thatcher famously got lost!

SHRIMP & CRAB LAYERED DIP

CATHY NEWBROUGH
LEBANON, MO

Delicious, but so simple to make! Great for office carry-in parties.

8-oz. pkg. cream cheese, softened
12-oz. bottle chili sauce
4-1/4 oz. can small shrimp, drained
4-1/4 oz. can crabmeat, drained and flaked
1 c. green pepper, chopped
5 to 6 green onions, chopped
3-oz. can sliced black olives, drained
1 to 2 8-oz. pkgs. shredded Cheddar cheese
snack crackers

Spread cream cheese on a snack plate; spread chili sauce over cream cheese. Sprinkle with shrimp, crabmeat and vegetables; top with shredded cheese. Cover and chill until serving time. Serve with crackers.

Serves 12

PRESENTATION

Add some vintage flair to your buffet by placing gently used game boards under your serving dishes. Check the closet for forgotten games or pick some up at yard sales. Cover with self-adhesive clear plastic for wipe-clean ease.

PUMPKIN PIE CHEESECAKE SPREAD

JENITA DAVISON
LA PLATA, MO

This spread is really good on vanilla wafers or graham crackers. All the spice of pumpkin pie, but so easy to mix, serve and eat! The spices can be adjusted to individual taste. Use dark brown sugar for a more intense flavor.

8-oz. pkg. cream cheese, softened
2 T. light brown sugar, packed
1/4 t. maple extract
1/4 t. cinnamon
1/4 t. nutmeg
1/8 t. ground ginger
1/8 t. ground cloves
graham crackers or vanilla wafers

In a bowl, with an electric mixer on medium speed, beat cream cheese until fluffy. Beat in brown sugar, extract and spices; transfer to a serving bowl. Cover and let stand for one hour before serving to allow flavors to combine. Serve with graham crackers or vanilla wafers.

Makes 12 servings

JALAPEÑO POPPERS

LAURA SMITH
APPLETON CITY, MO

We tried these yummy peppers on a camping trip with friends, and everyone loved them. Give it a try...I guarantee there will be none left!

20 jalapeño peppers, halved and seeds removed
2 8-oz. pkgs. cream cheese, softened
1 to 2 16-oz. pkgs. bacon

Fill each jalapeño half with cream cheese; wrap with a bacon slice and fasten with wooden toothpicks. Lay a long piece of aluminum foil on grill grate over medium heat; arrange peppers cheese-side up on foil. Cook until peppers are tender and bacon is crisp. Allow to cool slightly before serving. Poppers may also be placed on a rimmed baking sheet and baked at 350 degrees for 45 minutes.

Serves 8 to 10

CRISPY CHICKEN TASTIES

KELLY KOROKIS
FREDERICKTOWN, MO

My mom makes these appetizers for everything from family dinners to snacking while watching sports on television. We love 'em...they're even good cold!

1/2 c. lemon juice
3 T. soy sauce
1/2 t. salt
3 lbs. boneless, skinless chicken breasts, cut into 1-inch cubes
1 c. all-purpose flour
1 T. pepper
1/2 t. salt
1 T. paprika
peanut oil for frying

Mix lemon juice, soy sauce and salt together in a large bowl. Add chicken. Refrigerate for 3 hours, stirring occasionally. Drain, discarding marinade. Combine remaining ingredients except oil in a separate bowl. Coat chicken in flour mixture. Heat oil in a large skillet over medium-high heat. Add chicken; cook until golden on all sides and chicken juices run clear. Drain on paper towels before serving.

Serves 6 to 8

GREEN CHILE SOURDOUGH BITES

NAOMI TOWNSEND
OZARK, MO

We like to serve these tasty appetizers when our car club friends gather after a car show. I like to use small loaves of sourdough bread, sliced with an electric knife.

4-oz. can diced mild green chiles
1/2 c. butter, room temperature
1/2 c. mayonnaise
8-oz. pkg. shredded Monterey Jack cheese
1 loaf sourdough bread, cut into small bites
garlic powder to taste

In a bowl, mix chiles, butter and mayonnaise until smooth. Add cheese and stir to combine. Mixture may now be covered and refrigerated for later use. Spread chile mixture onto bread pieces. Arrange in a single layer on an aluminum foil-lined baking sheet. Sprinkle with garlic powder. Bake at 450 degrees until bubbly and crisp, about 3 to 4 minutes.

Serves 12

COUNTRY CAVIAR

KAY PYLE
STOCKTON, MO

One of our favorite dips! It's easy to make and keeps for days in the fridge, if it lasts that long. I have made it for ages and my grandkids love it. Great for family gatherings and football games. Spice it to suit to your taste, from mild to extra hot.

- **15-oz. can black, red or pinto beans, drained**
- **11-oz. can sweet corn & diced peppers, drained**
- **10-oz. can mild, medium or hot diced tomatoes with green chiles, drained**
- **6 green onions, chopped**
- **2 c. shredded Monterey Jack, Pepper Jack or Cheddar cheese**
- **1 c. light mayonnaise**
- **1 c. light sour cream**
- **hot pepper sauce to taste**
- **pita chips, tortilla chips**

Mix together all ingredients except chips in a large bowl. Cover and chill; may be kept refrigerated for several days. Serve with warm pita chips or tortilla chips.

Serves 8 to 10

RASPBERRY BRIE TARTS

DEBBIE CUTELLI
SAINT LOUIS, MO

These tarts look amazing on a holiday platter! I always keep the ingredients on hand to make this appetizer in case friends drop in.

- **2 2.1-oz. pkgs. frozen mini phyllo shells**
- **8-oz. round Brie cheese, cut into 1/2-inch cubes**
- **3 T. raspberry spreadable fruit**

Place phyllo shells on a large ungreased baking sheet. Place 3 cheese cubes into each shell. Bake at 350 degrees for 10 to 12 minutes, until cheese is melted and bubbly. Remove from oven. Spoon 1/4 teaspoon fruit over cheese in each shell. Return to oven; bake an additional 2 to 3 minutes, until heated through. Serve warm.

Makes 30

CHERYL'S AWESOME ARTICHOKE DIP

JUDY TAYLOR
BUTLER, MO

So simple to make, and so wonderful to eat, I'm so glad this recipe was shared with me! A small package of frozen chopped spinach may be thawed and added, if desired. Be sure to drain it well.

- **1 c. sour cream**
- **1 c. mayonnaise**
- **14-oz. can artichokes, drained and finely chopped**
- **6-oz. pkg. shredded Parmesan cheese**
- **1 t. garlic, minced**
- **crackers or bread slices**

Mix together all ingredients except crackers or bread in a mini slow cooker. Cover and cook on high setting for one to 2 hours, until bubbly and cheese has melted. Serve warm with crackers or bread for dipping.

Serves 8 to 10

ROBERT'S CORN DIP

CAROLE SNODGRASS
ROLLA, MO

This dip is sooo delicious! The flavor is even better if it's made 2 days ahead of time.

- **3 11-oz. cans sweet corn & diced peppers, drained**
- **7-oz. can chopped green chiles**
- **6-oz. can chopped jalapeños, drained and liquid added to taste**
- **1/2 c. green onion, chopped**
- **1 c. mayonnaise**
- **1 c. sour cream**
- **1 t. pepper**
- **1/2 t. garlic powder**
- **16-oz. pkg. shredded sharp Cheddar cheese**
- **corn chips**

Mix all ingredients except corn chips together and refrigerate. Serve with corn chips for scooping.

Makes 6 cups

CHEESY SPINACH-ARTICHOKE DIP

JUDY SCHERER
BENTON, MO

A slow-cooker recipe that's great for a party and really simple to make.

- 2 8-oz. pkgs. cream cheese, softened
- 3/4 c. half-and-half
- 10-oz. pkg. frozen chopped spinach, thawed and drained
- 13-oz. can artichoke hearts, drained and chopped
- 1 T. onion, finely chopped
- 1 clove garlic, minced
- 2/3 c. shredded Monterey Jack cheese
- 1/2 c. shredded Parmesan cheese
- tortilla chips or thin wheat crackers

In a large bowl, combine cream cheese and half-and-half; mix until well blended. Add spinach, artichokes, onion and garlic; stir well. Transfer mixture to a slow cooker. Cover and cook on high setting for 1-1/2 to 2 hours, until warmed through. At serving time, sprinkle with shredded cheeses. Serve with chips or crackers.

Makes 8 servings

KITCHEN TIP

A jar of dried, minced onion can be a real timesaver! If the recipe has a lot of liquid, such as soups and stews, it's easy to switch. Just substitute one tablespoon of dried, minced onion for every 1/3 cup fresh diced onion.

CHAPTER SIX

Silver Dollar

Desserts

THERE IS ALWAYS ROOM FOR DESSERT. SO WHEN YOUR SWEET TOOTH IS CALLING THESE SIMPLE SWEETS ARE THE PERFECT WAY TO END THE DAY.

ICE CREAM CAKE

D'ANN KOHLS
SPRINGFIELD, MO

This is my kids' favorite "cake." They request it every year for their birthdays!

- **16-oz. pkg. chocolate sandwich cookies, crushed**
- **1/4 c. margarine, melted**
- **1/2 gal. vanilla ice cream, softened**
- **11-3/4 oz. jar hot fudge sauce**
- **8-oz. container frozen whipped topping, thawed**

In a bowl, combine cookie crumbs with margarine. Press into the bottom of an ungreased 13"x9" baking pan. Spread ice cream over crust; cover and freeze until firm. Spread fudge sauce over ice cream; add whipped topping. Cover; freeze until firm. Remove from the freezer 5 minutes before serving.

Serves 12

APPLE-CRANBERRY PIE

SUSAN BICK
BALLWIN, MO

Serve slices of this delightful pie at your next holiday open house.

- **2 9-inch pie crusts, unbaked**
- **1-3/4 c. sugar**
- **1/4 c. all-purpose flour**
- **3 c. tart apples, cored, peeled and sliced**
- **2 c. cranberries**
- **2 T. butter, diced**

Line a 9" pie plate with one crust; set aside. Mix sugar and flour together. Alternate layers of apples, cranberries and sugar mixture in crust. Dot with butter; cover with remaining crust. Seal crusts together and cut small slits in top. Bake at 425 degrees for 40 to 50 minutes, or until crust is golden and juice begins to bubble through slits in crust.

Serves 6 to 8

PUMPKIN-CHOCOLATE CHIP COOKIES

CHRISTY MORRILL
LIBERTY, MO

These cookies were popular at a craft fair at our church years ago.

16-1/2 oz. pkg. spice cake mix
15-oz. can pumpkin
1 c. semi-sweet chocolate chips

In a bowl, combine dry cake mix, pumpkin and chocolate chips; mix well together. Scoop heaping tablespoonfuls of dough onto greased baking sheets. Bake at 350 degrees for 10 to 12 minutes, just until firm.

Makes 2 dozen

SAINT LOUIS GOOEY BUTTER CAKE

LINDA LESKO
SAINT LOUIS, MO

I grew up in Saint Louis, Missouri, and this was indeed my favorite dessert. Now living in Ilinois, I long for this dessert that no local bakery here makes. A good friend found this recipe, and it's as close as it gets. Enjoy!

18-1/2 oz. pkg. butter recipe yellow cake mix
4 eggs, divided
1/2 c. butter, softened
8-oz. pkg. cream cheese, room temperature
16-oz. pkg. powdered sugar

In a large bowl, combine cake mix, 2 eggs and butter. Beat with an electric mixer on medium speed for 2 minutes, or until well mixed. Pour batter into a well-greased and floured 13"x9" baking pan; set aside. In a separate bowl, beat together cream cheese, remaining eggs and powdered sugar until smooth. Spread over batter. Bake at 350 degrees for 40 to 45 minutes, until top is golden and edges are dark golden. Do not overbake.

Serves 10 to 12

GREAT-GRANDMA'S BLUE GOOSE PIE

JUDY TAYLOR
BUTLER, MO

My mother-in-law is a fabulous cook and her kitchen table has been a haven of comfort for many years. After raising five children, she hasn't slowed down...if anything, she's become busier! Her children, grandchildren and now great-grandchildren are treated often to her tasty homemade cooking like this yummy berry pie.

2 9-inch pie crusts, unbaked
2-1/2 to 3 c. sugar, divided
3 c. gooseberries
1 c. blueberries
3 T. instant tapioca
Garnish: water, 2 t. sugar

Place one pie crust in a 9" pie plate; sprinkle with 2 tablespoons sugar and set aside. Mix together berries and remaining sugar in a microwave-safe bowl. Microwave on high setting for about 5 minutes, checking often, until berries start to pop open. Transfer berry mixture to pie crust. Cover with top crust; crimp to seal and cut small slits in crust. Sprinkle crust with a little water and then sprinkle with sugar. Bake at 350 degrees until golden, about 45 minutes.

Serves 5 to 6

PRESENTATION

If you're planning a family gathering, decorate your table to bring back childhood memories. Glue photocopies of old family photos to heavy paper for personalized table centerpieces.

BAKE-SALE BUTTERSCOTCH BARS

LINDA EIVINS
BLYTHEDALE, MO

My mom always made these delicious cookie bars for me to take to bake sales while they were still warm from the oven.

1/2 c. butter
2 c. brown sugar, packed
2 eggs
1 t. vanilla extract
2 c. all-purpose flour
2 t. baking powder
1/4 t. salt
1 c. sweetened flaked coconut
1 c. chopped walnuts

In a saucepan over low heat, combine butter and brown sugar. Cook until bubbly, stirring constantly. Allow to cool. Add eggs to mixture, one at a time; beat well after each addition. Stir in vanilla. Sift together flour, baking powder and salt; add to butter mixture along with coconut and nuts. Mix thoroughly; spread into a greased 15"x10" jelly-roll pan. Bake at 350 degrees for about 25 minutes. Cut into bars while still warm. Remove from pan when almost cooled.

Makes 3 dozen

STARLIGHT MINT SURPRISES

MARY GOURLEY
FLORISSANT, MO

This recipe was given to me by my mother. She always made these special cookies at Christmastime...they bring back great memories!

3 c. all-purpose flour
1 t. baking soda
1/2 t. salt
1 c. butter, softened
1 c. sugar
1/2 c. brown sugar, packed
2 eggs
2 T. water
1 t. vanilla extract
9-oz. pkg. chocolate mint wafer candies
72 walnut halves

Sift together flour, baking soda and salt; set aside. In a separate bowl, beat butter until creamy; gradually beat in sugars. Blend well. Add eggs, one at a time; beat well after each addition. Add water and vanilla; stir well. Add flour mixture to butter mixture; mix thoroughly. Cover and refrigerate for at least 2 hours. Press about 1-1/2 tablespoons of dough around each wafer to cover completely. Place on greased baking sheets, about 2 inches apart. Top each cookie with a walnut half. Bake at 375 degrees for 10 to 12 minutes.

Makes about 6 dozen

RITZY FRUIT COBBLER

SUE MORRISON
BLUE SPRING, MO

This is an original recipe of mine. It's a very good way to use up odds & ends of frozen fruit.

- **4 c. frozen blueberries, cherries, blackberries, strawberries, raspberries, sliced peaches or a mixture, divided**
- **1 c. sugar, divided**
- **1 sleeve round buttery crackers, divided**
- **2 T. butter, softened**
- **Optional: cinnamon to taste**
- **juice of 1 lemon**
- **Garnish: vanilla ice cream**

Spray a slow cooker with non-stick vegetable spray. Add one cup frozen fruit; sprinkle with 1/4 cup sugar. Arrange 8 whole crackers on top. Continue layering, making 3 more layers of fruit, sugar and crackers. For top layer, crush remaining crackers; mix with butter and remaining sugar. Sprinkle cracker mixture on top; add cinnamon, if desired. Sprinkle with lemon juice. Cover and cook on low setting for one to 1-1/2 hours, until bubbly and fruit is juicy. Stir gently, breaking up crackers; the crackers will thicken the mixture. Serve warm from slow cooker, topped with a scoop of ice cream.

Makes 4 to 6 servings

KITCHEN TIP

A pinch of ground cloves brings out the flavor in cinnamon-sugar.

PEANUT BUTTER POPCORN

AMY TEETS
O'FALLON, MO

This recipe was handed down from a friend of the family. If you like, when you're done mixing, bake the popcorn on an ungreased baking sheet at 200 degrees for 20 minutes.

2 3-1/2 oz. pkgs. microwave popcorn, popped
1/2 c. margarine
3/4 c. brown sugar, packed
20 marshmallows
1/4 c. creamy peanut butter

Place popcorn into a large bowl; set aside. In a separate microwave-safe bowl, combine margarine, brown sugar and marshmallows. Microwave on high at one-minute intervals, stirring between each interval, until mixture is melted and smooth. Stir in peanut butter until well blended. Pour margarine mixture over popcorn; stir quickly to coat before it cools.

Serves 8

COCONUT-ORANGE RICE PUDDING

SHARON CRIDER
JUNCTION CITY, MO

It's easy to keep the ingredients on hand for this yummy pudding.

11-oz. can mandarin oranges, drained and syrup reserved
3-1/2 c. milk
3-1/4 oz. pkg. cook & serve coconut cream pudding mix
1/2 c. instant rice, uncooked

Combine reserved syrup, milk and dry pudding mix in a saucepan. Stir in rice. Cook over medium heat until mixture comes to a boil, about 5 minutes. Cover and let stand for 5 minutes. Divide into serving dishes; garnish with orange sections. Cover and chill until serving time.

Makes 8 servings

APPLE SPICE CAKE

MARIE KING
INDEPENDENCE, MO

One day I wanted some of my grandma's applesauce raisin spice cookies, but didn't want to make cookies. So I started adding ingredients and came up with this recipe. It was a huge hit! It is really good warm, right out of the oven...even better the next day!

18-1/4 oz. pkg. spice cake mix
15-oz. can unsweetened applesauce
2 eggs, beaten
1 Gala apple, peeled, cored and diced
1/2 c. raisins
1/4 c. pecans, chopped

In a large bowl, beat together dry cake mix, applesauce and eggs. Stir in apple, raisins and pecans. Mix until combined. Spread batter evenly in a greased 13"x9" glass baking pan. Bake at 350 degrees for 45 to 50 minutes. Cake will be moist and not quite done in the very center. Remove from oven; let cool for 5 minutes. Meanwhile, make Vanilla-Caramel Glaze; drizzle over warm cake. Let cool for 25 to 30 minutes before serving.

Vanilla-Caramel Glaze:

Vanilla-Caramel Glaze

3/4 c. powdered sugar
1 T. caramel ice cream topping
1-1/2 t. vanilla extract
2 to 4 T. water

Combine powdered sugar, topping and vanilla; mix well. Stir in water, one tablespoon at a time, until glaze coats the back of spoon.

Serves 20

GRANDMA POWER'S OATMEAL CAKE

TERRI LOCK
CARROLLTON, MO

This recipe is like a warm pudding...great to enjoy on a cold winter day! My grandmother shared so much love with her family and especially when she baked her wonderful desserts.

- **1 c. long-cooking oats, uncooked**
- **1-1/2 c. water**
- **1/2 c. plus 2 T. butter, softened and divided**
- **1 c. sugar**
- **1-3/4 c. brown sugar, packed and divided**
- **2 eggs**
- **1-1/3 c. all-purpose flour**
- **1 t. baking soda**
- **1/2 t. salt**
- **1/2 t. cinnamon**
- **1/4 c. evaporated milk**
- **1/4 c. sweetened flaked coconut**

Cook oats with water as directed on package; set aside to cool. In a bowl, blend together 1/2 cup butter, sugar and 3/4 cup brown sugar; stir in eggs, one at a time. In a separate bowl, sift together flour, baking soda, salt and cinnamon. Add flour mixture to butter mixture alternately with oat mixture; stir well. Pour batter into a 9" deep-dish pie plate. Bake, uncovered, at 350 degrees for one hour. Meanwhile, in a separate bowl, mix together remaining butter, remaining brown sugar, evaporated milk and coconut. Spread on cake. Broil cake until topping is bubbly and golden.

Serves 6 to 8

PRESENTATION

Wrap sandwiches for your garden party in wax paper and tie with a length of gingham ribbon. Serve them in a favorite basket lined with a vintage tea towel.

MOM'S 75-DOLLAR PECAN PIE

SYLVIA RATLEY
BRANSON, MO

Lots of bakers have a great pecan pie recipe, but this one is firmer and not as gooey as most. My 93-year-old mom got this recipe over 50 years ago from a dear friend at church and added her special touches. This pie was recently auctioned at my sister's school for 75 dollars. Enjoy!

- **3/4 c. sugar**
- **3/4 c. dark corn syrup**
- **1-1/2 T. all-purpose flour**
- **1-1/2 to 2 T. butter, melted and slightly cooled**
- **3 eggs, beaten**
- **1 t. vanilla extract**
- **1 c. pecan halves**
- **9-inch pie crust, unbaked**

Combine all ingredients except pecans and pie crust in a large bowl. Mix well; stir in pecans. Pour mixture into unbaked pie crust. Bake at 325 degrees for 40 to 50 minutes, until golden and a knife tip inserted in the center comes out clean. Cool before slicing.

Serves 6 to 8

MAPLE SUGAR COOKIES

MICHELLE CRABTREE
LEE'S SUMMIT, MO

Use only pure maple syrup for the yummiest flavor.

- **1 c. butter-flavored shortening**
- **1-1/4 c. sugar**
- **2 eggs**
- **1/4 c. maple syrup**
- **1 T. vanilla extract**
- **3 c. all-purpose flour**
- **3/4 t. baking powder**
- **1/2 t. baking soda**
- **1/2 t. salt**

Blend together shortening and sugar. Add eggs, one at a time, beating well after each addition. Beat in syrup and vanilla. In a separate bowl, combine remaining ingredients; gradually add to shortening mixture. Cover and refrigerate for 2 hours, or until easy to handle. On a lightly floured surface, roll out to 1/8-inch thick. Cut with a 2-1/2 inch cookie cutter dipped in flour. Arrange on ungreased baking sheets one inch apart. Bake at 375 degrees for 8 to 10 minutes, until golden. Remove to wire rack; cool.

Makes 2 dozen

PECAN OZARKS

MARIAN FORCK
CHAMOIS, MO

My Great-Aunt Anna gave this recipe to me. She was a very special lady and had a heart of gold. She had many nieces and nephews and was loved by all.

4 egg whites
1-1/2 c. sugar
1 t. vanilla extract
1-1/2 c. chopped pecans
Optional: 1/2 c. chopped dates

Combine egg whites and sugar in a saucepan. Whisk together over low heat just until warmed. Transfer mixture to a bowl. With an electric mixer on high speed, beat mixture until stiff peaks form. Stir in vanilla; fold in pecans and dates, if desired. Drop by teaspoonfuls onto greased baking sheets. Bake at 325 degrees for 12 minutes. Allow cookies to cool on baking sheets before removing.

Makes 5 dozen

SAUCEPAN COOKIES

JULIE HAGEN
SPRINGFIELD, MO

Serious comfort food! I come from a large family in Maine...on cold winter days, these cookies were so much fun to make and eat.

1/2 c. butter
2 1-oz. sqs. unsweetened baking chocolate
1/2 c. milk
2 c. sugar
1/2 t. salt
1 t. vanilla extract
4 c. quick-cooking oats, uncooked

In a heavy saucepan over medium heat, melt butter and chocolate. Add milk, sugar and salt. Bring to a boil; boil for 2 minutes. Remove from heat. Add vanilla and oats; mix well. Drop by rounded tablespoonfuls onto wax paper to cool.

Makes 4 dozen

GRANDMA FRY'S NANAIMO BARS

STELLA JENSEN
CAPE GIRARDEAU, MO

A Canadian treat. My mother always made these for special occasions when I was growing up, and now I make them to remember her by.

- **1 c. plus 1 T. butter, softened and divided**
- **1/4 c. sugar**
- **1-oz. sq. unsweetened baking chocolate, chopped**
- **1 t. vanilla extract**
- **1 egg, beaten**
- **2 c. graham cracker crumbs**
- **1/2 c. chopped nuts**
- **1 c. sweetened flaked coconut**
- **2 T. instant vanilla pudding mix**
- **2 c. powdered sugar**
- **3 T. milk**
- **4 1-oz. sqs. semi-sweet baking chocolate, chopped**

Combine 1/2 cup butter, sugar and unsweetened chocolate in a double boiler over medium heat. Cook until well blended; stir in vanilla. Add egg; cook for 5 minutes. Remove from heat; stir in crumbs, nuts and coconut. Press into a greased 13"x9" baking pan; chill for 15 minutes. Beat 1/2 cup butter until fluffy; stir in pudding mix, powdered sugar and milk. Spread over mixture. Melt semi-sweet chocolate and remaining butter over low heat until well blended. Spread over top; chill before cutting into bars.

Makes 3 dozen

APPLEDOODLES

KATIE WOLLGAST
TROY, MO

Snickerdoodles have been one of my favorites since my kindergarten teacher used to make them for us. This is a wonderful twist. They are so good in fall, served warm with a cold glass of milk. Rolling the little balls is fun for children and children at heart!

2-2/3 c. all-purpose flour
2 t. baking powder
1 t. cream of tartar
1/2 t. salt
1/2 t. cinnamon
1/2 t. nutmeg
1/2 c. butter, softened
3/4 c. sugar, divided
1/2 c. brown sugar, packed
2 eggs, beaten
1 t. vanilla extract
1 c. tart apple, peeled and shredded
1/2 c. walnuts, finely chopped
2 t. apple pie spice or additional cinnamon

In a bowl, combine flour, baking powder, cream of tartar, salt and spices; set aside. In a large bowl, blend butter, 1/2 cup sugar and brown sugar. Beat in eggs and vanilla. Add flour mixture to butter mixture; stir until moistened. Stir in apple and nuts. Combine remaining sugar and spice in a small bowl; set aside. With floured hands, roll dough into 48 smooth balls, about one inch. Coat balls with sugar mixture. Place balls on parchment paper-lined baking sheets, 2 inches apart. Bake at 350 degrees for 12 to 15 minutes, until lightly golden on the edges and barely set in the centers. Cool for 2 minutes; remove to wire racks to cool completely.

Makes 4 dozen

RED VELVET CAKE

ANGELA MILLER
JEFFERSON CITY, MO

My grandma and aunt make this wonderful cake for my birthday in November and I usually make it again for Christmas. The homemade frosting is scrumptious...well worth the time!

18-1/4 oz. pkg. fudge marble cake mix
1 t. baking soda
2 eggs, beaten
1-1/2 c. buttermilk
1-oz. bottle red food coloring
1 t. vanilla extract

Combine dry cake mix and baking soda in a medium bowl; add remaining ingredients. Blend with an electric mixer on low speed until moistened. Beat on high speed for 2 minutes. Pour batter into 2 greased and floured 9" round cake pans. Bake at 350 degrees for 30 to 35 minutes, until cake tests done. Cool in pans for 10 minutes; turn out onto a wire rack. Cool completely; if desired, freeze layers overnight to make cake easier to frost. Frost between layers, top and sides of cake. If frozen, thaw one hour before serving.

Vanilla Frosting:

VANILLA FROSTING
5 T. all-purpose flour
1 c. milk
1 c. butter, softened
1 c. sugar
2 t. vanilla extract

Whisk flour and milk in a saucepan over medium-low heat until smooth. Bring to a boil; cook and stir for 2 minutes, or until thickened. Cover and refrigerate. In a medium bowl, blend butter and sugar; add chilled milk mixture. Beat for 10 minutes, or until fluffy. Stir in vanilla.

Serves 10-12

JUST FOR FUN

Missouri is one of two states with an official State Grape. Missouri's State Grape is Norton/Cynthiana grape.

GREAT-GRANDMA MUSSELMAN'S COOKIES

JOYCE KEELING
MANSFIELD, MO

It wouldn't be Christmas without my Great-Grandma Musselman's ginger cookies. She always baked these cookies for Christmas and they always had to have pink frosting. They stay soft in a tightly covered container for weeks...if they last that long!

1 c. sugar
1 c. shortening
2 eggs, beaten
1 c. molasses
5 c. all-purpose flour
1 t. cinnamon
2 t. ground ginger
1 T. baking soda
2 T. hot water
1 T. vinegar

FLUFFY FROSTING
1 egg white, beaten
2 T. sugar
1/8 t. salt
1/2 c. light corn syrup
1/2 t. vanilla extract
1 drop red food coloring

In a large bowl, blend together sugar and shortening. Beat in eggs, molasses, flour and spices. Dissolve baking soda in hot water; stir in vinegar and add to flour mixture. Divide dough into thirds and roll out on a lightly floured surface to about 1/8-inch thickness. Cut out with round cookie cutters and arrange on an ungreased baking sheet. Bake at 350 degrees for 10 minutes, or until very lightly golden around edges. Cool; frost with Fluffy Frosting.

Fluffy Frosting:

Combine all ingredients except vanilla and food coloring in a double-boiler over medium heat. Heat water in bottom of double-boiler over medium-high heat; do not bring water to a boil Using an electric mixer, beat mixture 8 minutes, or until stiff peaks form. Remove from heat; stir in vanilla and food coloring to tint a soft pink. Beat until thick enough to spread.

Makes 6 dozen

CRANBERRY CARAMEL CAKE

DEBBIE CUTELLI
SAINT LOUIS, MO

This cake is great any time of the day. Who doesn't love pumpkin and cranberries during the holidays? The caramel sauce makes it extra special.

18-1/4 oz. pkg. yellow cake mix with pudding
4 eggs, beaten
1 c. eggnog
1/3 c. oil
2 t. pumpkin pie spice
1-1/2 c. fresh or frozen cranberries, chopped
1 c. chopped walnuts

In a large bowl, combine dry cake mix, eggs, eggnog, oil and spice. Beat with an electric mixer on low speed for 30 seconds; beat for 2 minutes on medium speed. Fold in cranberries and walnuts. Pour batter into a greased and lightly floured 12-cup fluted tube pan. Bake at 350 degrees for 45 to 55 minutes, until a toothpick inserted near center comes out clean. Cool in pan for 10 minutes. Invert cake onto a wire rack; remove pan and cool for about one hour. Drizzle warm Caramel Sauce over cake before serving.

Caramel Sauce:

Caramel Sauce
1/2 c. butter
1-1/4 c. brown sugar, packed
2 T. light corn syrup
1/2 c. whipping cream

Melt butter in a saucepan over medium-high heat. Stir in brown sugar and corn syrup; bring to a boil. Cook for one minute or until sugar dissolves, stirring constantly. Stir in cream. Return to a boil, stirring constantly. Remove from heat.

Serves 16

165-DOLLAR BLACKBERRY-APPLE PIE

MARIAN FORCK
CHAMOIS, MO

My husband Bernie makes this every year for the Frankenstein, Missouri Fall Supper pie auction. One year it went for 165 dollars! They ask him to make it again every year.

- **2 9-inch pie crusts, unbaked**
- **2-1/2 lbs. Gala apples, peeled, cored and sliced**
- **2 c. frozen blackberries**
- **1 c. sugar**
- **2 T. all-purpose flour**
- **1 to 2 t. cinnamon**
- **1/2 t. nutmeg**
- **1 T. butter, diced**
- **Garnish: additional sugar and cinnamon**
- **Optional: vanilla ice cream**

Place one pie crust in a 9" pie plate; set aside. In a bowl, combine apples, blackberries, sugar, flour and spices. Toss to mix; spoon into crust. Dot pie with butter; top with remaining crust. Pinch edges to seal and cut vents; decorate with crust cut-outs, if desired. Sprinkle with additional sugar and cinnamon if desired. Bake at 375 degrees for one to 1-1/2 hours, until fruit is bubbly and top crust is golden. Serve topped with ice cream, if desired.

Serves 6 to 8

DINNERTIME CONVERSATION

Earthquakes aren't just for California. Four of the largest in North American history... up to a moment magnitude of 8.0, occurred from December 1811 to February 1812 in New Madrid, Missouri.

FRESH STRAWBERRY PIE

EVA JO HOYLE
MEXICO, MO

My family loves strawberries in the springtime. I love to make this fresh strawberry pie for them.

- **1-1/2 c. water**
- **1 c. sugar**
- **3 T. cornstarch**
- **1/8 t. salt**
- **3-oz. pkg. strawberry gelatin mix**
- **1 T. lemon juice**
- **1 t. red food coloring**
- **4 c. fresh strawberries, hulled and sliced**
- **9-inch pie crust, baked, or graham cracker crust**
- **Optional: whipped cream**

In a saucepan over medium heat, combine water, sugar, cornstarch and salt. Bring to a boil. Boil for 3 to 4 minutes, until mixture is clear. Stir in dry gelatin mix, lemon juice and food coloring. Remove from heat and set aside to cool. Arrange strawberries in baked crust. Pour cooled gelatin mixture over berries. Cover and refrigerate until set. Top with whipped cream, if desired.

Serves 8

INDEX

Mains

Salads

U.S. to METRIC RECIPE EQUIVALENTS

Volume Measurements

¼ teaspoon	1 mL
½ teaspoon	2 mL
1 teaspoon	5 mL
1 tablespoon = 3 teaspoons	15 mL
2 tablespoons = 1 fluid ounce	30 mL
¼ cup	60 mL
⅓ cup	75 mL
½ cup = 4 fluid ounces	125 mL
1 cup = 8 fluid ounces	250 mL
2 cups = 1 pint = 16 fluid ounces	500 mL
4 cups = 1 quart	1 L

Weights

1 ounce	30 g
4 ounces	120 g
8 ounces	225 g
16 ounces = 1 pound	450 g

Baking Pan Sizes

Square

8x8x2 inches	2 L = 20x20x5 cm
9x9x2 inches	2.5 L = 23x23x5 cm

Rectangular

13x9x2 inches	3.5 L = 33x23x5 cm

Loaf

9x5x3 inches	2 L = 23x13x7 cm

Round

8x1½ inches	1.2 L = 20x4 cm
9x1½ inches	1.5 L = 23x4 cm

Recipe Abbreviations

t. = teaspoon	ltr. = liter
T. = tablespoon	oz. = ounce
c. = cup	lb. = pound
pt. = pint	doz. = dozen
qt. = quart	pkg. = package
gal. = gallon	env. = envelope

Oven Temperatures

300° F.	150° C
325° F.	160° C
350° F.	180° C
375° F.	190° C
400° F.	200° C
450° F.	230° C

Kitchen Measurements

A pinch = ⅛ tablespoon
1 fluid ounce = 2 tablespoons
3 teaspoons = 1 tablespoon
4 fluid ounces = ½ cup
2 tablespoons = ⅛ cup
8 fluid ounces = 1 cup
4 tablespoons = ¼ cup
16 fluid ounces = 1 pint
8 tablespoons = ½ cup
32 fluid ounces = 1 quart
16 tablespoons = 1 cup
16 ounces net weight = 1 pound
2 cups = 1 pint
4 cups = 1 quart
4 quarts = 1 gallon